STARGATE ATLANTIS

THE OFFICIAL COMPANION

SEASON 2

STARGATE: ATLANTIS: THE OFFICIAL COMPANION SEASON 2

ISBN: 1 84576 163 4
ISBN-13: 978 1 84576 163 9

Published by
Titan Books
A division of
Titan Publishing Group Ltd
144 Southwark St
London
SE1 0UP

First edition July 2006
2 4 6 8 10 9 7 5 3 1

Stargate: Atlantis: The Official Companion Season Two © 2006 Metro-Goldwyn-Mayer Studios Inc.
All Rights Reserved.
STARGATE: ATLANTIS © 2004-2006 MGM Global Holdings Inc.
STARGATE: ATLANTIS is a trademark of Metro-Goldwyn-Mayer Studios Inc. All Rights Reserved.

DEDICATION

For the cast, crew, and producers of *Stargate: Atlantis*, too numerous to name but every one indispensable.
Thanks for a great show!

ACKNOWLEDGEMENTS

First and foremost, thank you to executive producers Brad Wright and Robert C. Cooper, whose continued support
is overwhelming and very much appreciated. Thanks too to all the producers, writers and directors — Joseph
Mallozzi, Paul Mullie, Martin Wood, Martin Gero, Peter DeLuise, Damian Kindler, Andy Mikita, Carl Binder —
for your input and help in putting this volume together (hope I didn't forget anyone). Huge thanks to the cast,
particularly Torri Higginson for providing such a lovely Foreword. Thanks also to Martin Gero for the Afterword.
Thanks to Brigitte Prochaska and Carol Appleby at Bridge Studios and Karol Mora at MGM for all your hard work
and dedication — this definitely couldn't have been done without you. Thanks to Bruce Woloshyn at Rainmaker
for providing us with such wonderful pictures. Finally, thank you to Jo Boylett, my editor at Titan Books,
for making sure this book is readable!

Titan Books would also like to thank all the *Stargate: Atlantis* cast and crew. We're also grateful to
Karol Mora at MGM for her continuing help and to Bruce G. Woloshyn at Rainmaker Animation &
Visual Effects.

Did you enjoy this book? We love to hear from our readers. Please e-mail us at: **readerfeedback@titanemail.com**
or write to Reader Feedback at the above address. To subscribe to our regular newsletter for up-to-the-minute
news, great offers and competitions, email: **titan-news@titanemail.com**

Visit our website: **www.titanbooks.com**

A CIP catalogue record for this title is available from the British Library.

Printed in Canada

THE OFFICIAL COMPANION

SEASON 2   SHARON GOSLING

STARGATE: ATLANTIS DEVELOPED FOR TELEVISION BY
BRAD WRIGHT AND ROBERT C. COOPER

TITAN BOOKS

CONTENTS

FOREWORD

oreword means 'first word' or 'the word in front', doesn't it? (For the sake of this little stream of consciousness, let's presume it does.) Well now, to write a first word about *Stargate: Atlantis* would be impossible; there have already been so many words written about *Stargate SG-1* and now *Stargate: Atlantis*. So all I can hope to offer is to contribute to the middle words! I know it can't be the last word — this is partly because of hope, but mostly I *know* this because we are presently shooting season three. So hopefully there will be at least one more 'last word' Foreword — and, in fact, I hope for many more middle words before that last word is written…

Here we are, all who are reading this, looking over season two of *Atlantis*, so my first pointed middle word must be: thanks. Thank you for watching us (and reading this), for without you there would be no us. Eternal gratitude. Because of all of you, I get to have one of the coolest jobs around. Not only because I get to be the boss of a team of scintillating and handsome hero boys, and not just because they *have* to listen to me even though I don't carry a gun. Not only because I have the joy of having the strong, smart and lovely Rachel to giggle with. But also because a lot of science fiction acting takes place entirely in your imagination.

Now, I recall acting teachers pounding into my head how I should "Never 'act' only 're-act'". Well, at the start of the first season I was cursing them, thinking, "What the hell do I do? My reaction to a big piece of green fabric isn't going to be that interesting!" And then the fear surfaces that if it isn't connected to your heart, you will end up in the "no turn un-stoned" school of over-over-acting. Then, somewhere along the way, I remembered play. As a kid you don't need anything but your own belief in the story you are living out. You don't worry about props or logic or even if your sister knows she's playing the part of the Evil Guardian of the Treasure who you have to sneak past to get to the Kitchen of Gold. It's your world you create and every inch of it feels real. So now I get paid to play. And play all day is exactly what we do!

There are days on set when we get tired and grumpy or frustrated with solving problems, be it props or blocking or words, but almost immediately we look around and remember — or sometimes are reminded — how lucky we all are. Not only are the people surrounding me each day so talented, funny and, on the whole, kind, but this entire franchise has inspired such creativity and connection from its loyal viewers. Some of the art I've been sent and scripts I've read from fans online are treasures. People like Sharon (Gosling, the loyal author of this series of companions, among many other *Stargate* words written) put so much into this. So alongside 'The Powers That Be', Brad Wright and Robert Cooper — for starting this whole damn thing and giving me a job in their self-made madness — all our wonderful writers, directors, magician DOPs, cast, every one of our incredible crew, and my sister for giving me all that practice as a kid, I must thank all of you for this really great part of my life.

I didn't grow up on science fiction, in fact I never really got it. So when I was offered

a job on *Stargate: Atlantis* it meant a crash course in sci-fi. And phew! What a course it was... (I only wish this companion had been available then. Where were you Sharon?) I soon discovered some of the many things I would come to love about it. For one, how it creates a safe haven to explore politics and philosophies which may be too delicate to ponder overtly and explicitly at certain times in history. But maybe more precious is its ability to bring strangers and outsiders together — both in other galaxies and right here at home.

Sci-fi fans are one of a kind: loyal, detail oriented ("in episode three the button to the left was pressed to engage the ZPM reset, and in episode nine someone pressed the right button") — alright, some are a bit obsessive — and all of them are open of heart. The number of letters I've received from people telling me how they met their best friends in sci-fi chat rooms, and some even sharing how they found the loves of their lives at conventions, blows my mind. And it was that same impulse that made my character, Dr Elizabeth Weir, take the job as head of the Pegasus Galaxy expedition: to explore different cultures, find the similarities... and celebrate the differences (well mainly — when the Wraith come to visit we don't put out the chips and dip). So far she's met with more defensive than open cultures... but she, like I, believes there is more good than bad out there. And so we both hope for future Forewords in future companions on future *Atlantis* seasons. Å

TORRI HIGGINSON
Vancouver, May 2006

THE
JOURNEY
CONTINUES

INTO SEASON 2

"They found a way to soup up their space guns."
— Sheppard

With the success of *Stargate: Atlantis'* first year came the promise of a second, which needed to be even bigger, better and more exciting than its predecessor. As the cast, crew and production were all still glowing from the knowledge that they were able to pull off a great season of television, everyone was raring to go for year two. Before they could do so, though, the producers had to develop a framework for the season — and deal with several changes that were to alter the very fabric of the series.

The biggest decision during the development of season two was to reduce the amount of time that Lieutenant Aiden Ford (Rainbow Sun Francks) spent on screen. As often happens during the first 'shakedown' season of a show, the producers had realized that for some indefinable reason, the character wasn't quite working as they had planned. If they were going to make a significant change, then season two was the perfect opportunity to do so. "You have to sit down at the end of each season and say, 'What worked, what didn't work, and how can we fix it?'" explains producer Martin Gero. "Rainbow is a really good actor, [but] it was a vicious circle where that character did not get developed to anyone's content; Rainbow wasn't happy, we weren't happy, the network wasn't happy."

"It's a question of the character not readily fulfilling the dynamic we were looking for," continues Brad Wright candidly, "which was to provide a sort of sidekick to Sheppard, so that we could have witty banter, a back and forth between the two of them as evidenced in the pilot. But Rainbow didn't quite gel in that respect as much as David [Hewlett] did with Joe [Flanigan], and *he* became a source of the banter, so many of the episodes became a McKay-Sheppard thing. And so we, as writers, started leaving Ford out of that equation, which is unfair to the actor, because how can he make something out of nothing?"

For director and producer Martin Wood (who filmed Janet Fraiser's momentous death several years earlier for *Stargate SG-1*) there was another reason entirely for altering the balance of characters in *Stargate: Atlantis*. "I know what the reasoning is on both sides, for keeping and for letting a main character go," explains the director. "I've said this any number of times — I *believe* in letting main characters go, because there's jeopardy then. You have to do that, otherwise every situation you get into, it's like, 'Yeah, and we know they're going to be back next week.' But if you get rid of some of the lead characters, it amps up the jeopardy for the rest of the team. So now, any time you go into something, it's dangerous. So that's how I was feeling about it, 'Good, we're putting a main character's life on the line and that's important.'"

Unwilling to simply write the character out of the series permanently, the writing

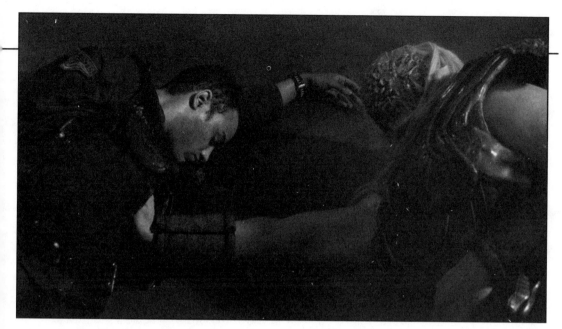

team sat down and worked to come up with a solution that would allow the character to stay in the Pegasus Galaxy whilst also completely redesigning his input into the show.

"The hardest part about this is that we all love Rainbow," says Gero. "Personally I was very friendly with him, because we are the same age, and we both moved out here at the same time. So we said, 'We think we can do this a lot better, but you're going to have to take a step back,' and would he be willing to do that? Because part of it was his decision as well, because he might have said no, and then we would have been screwed because it would have been like, 'Well do we cut the character entirely or what?' We came up with a really cool idea of what to do with Ford's character. It meant a massive reduction in role, and we were nervous about what Rainbow would think, but we were really surprised and pleased that he was actually excited about it. I think he felt that he was underused, and he didn't feel that anymore. He's the epicenter of four episodes. Not only that, the bad part about being on a show like this is that you have no time to do anything else. So this freed him up creatively to focus on his music career and on other acting gigs. So the whole thing actually turned into something very exciting that all parties were very happy with."

"We realized that the only way to do the character justice was to transform him," recalls Wright, "and that's why I pitched this idea of him being affected by a feeding to the point where it screwed with his mind and changed him physiologically."

Unusually, the producers and writers also asked for the actor's input, asking what direction Francks would like to see his character move towards. "I wanted him to be crazy," Francks recalls. "I just thought that one of the things that he should have was a healing factor, somehow, and [have him] become almost like a super-soldier. Then Brad had the great idea with the Wraith stuff. Initially it was to make him part-Wraith, [but we couldn't] do that because it just brought up too many things for the future, so we made it a totally random occurrence. No one knows what happens to a human when they're getting the life sucked out of them by the Wraith. So have the Wraith suddenly die! Then we created this enzyme and it became just all these ideas. And that's it, that's how he was born. I wanted an actual physical change, so I was big on the eye."

"The 'one eye' thing was just an image I had," says Wright. "I had no idea why that happened, but it's cool, isn't it?" he laughs.

"They originally wanted me to have one Wraith eye," Francks recalls, "but I thought it would be much better to have something completely different, because I'm human, I'm not a Wraith. I wanted it to be more random, so then we came up with the all-black — I like to call it the 'shark' — eye. It was cool, because that eye is completely emotionless. If your eyes are the window to your soul, then he's almost soulless on the left side of his body. It's almost like a *Batman* Two-Face sort of thing that was going on. And then there was the aging, which we see happen when you are being attacked by the Wraith. We aged the side of his face — that was pretty cool. From far away, it just looks like he's scarred, but really he's aged. Todd Masters just did a wonderful job in the rendering of the aging of my face," laughs Francks. "I was like, 'Oh my God, is that what I'm going to look like?'"

Below: The beginning of season two had its fair share of shocks for the audience.

In the end, the transformation of Ford from loyal soldier to pumped-up renegade was, by all accounts, the best thing that had ever happened to the character. It gave Rainbow Sun Francks an acting role he could really sink his teeth into, it gave the writers

a virtually new character to write for, and it introduced a sense of jeopardy for the team. "Once we came up with the idea, it was so exciting," Gero smiles. "It's hard... When we go up against the Genii, we have a history with them, but if it ever got bad, we wouldn't hesitate to kill Ladon, for example. But no matter how bad Ford gets, Sheppard is always going to hesitate to kill him. I was reading comic books recently, and one of the archetypes that comes through is the hero and his fallen brother. You get real drama out of two guys, one driven by a pure moral compass and one who for whatever reason goes to the dark side. You're not able to vilify Ford as quickly as you could Ladon, because we're connected to him. So the type of stories you can tell about that conflict within Sheppard and the rest of the team are really interesting. Something that was a weakness on the show has now become a strength."

Having solved the problem of how to reinvigorate the character of Aiden Ford, the producers were left with another issue. They still needed a character to provide a sidekick for Joe Flanigan's character, John Sheppard. Having someone to play against was a vital facet of the Sheppard character, and although, as Wright observed, they had discovered a natural banter between Sheppard and David Hewlett's McKay, they still needed someone else. Deciding who was a major part of Brad Wright and Robert Cooper's pre-season planning, made all the more urgent because not only did they have to work out the character they wanted, they also had to cast the role.

"We talked about a lot of different versions," says executive producer Robert Cooper, "a lot of different scenarios. I think it's okay for me to say that Brad and I probably disagreed a bit about how to go with the Ronon character. Brad wanted him to be a military guy, and I wanted him to be this very 'rough around the edges' alien. The Ronon you finally end up seeing in season two is a compromise of the two, and I think he's very cool. He's a rough around the edges alien with a great backstory who also was a military man, and thus is able to fall into his role with the team in a believable way."

"We were debating long about who he was going to be," agrees Wright. "And it's funny, I've been doing this long enough to know that it's very important to have an idea of what you want to do, but it's more important to cast somebody who remotely fits that idea. What we realized the series was lacking was somebody who, just with a look or by stepping into the room, had a threatening or dangerous presence. If, going into a fight, you always thought that Teyla was the one who was going to watch our backs, then you've got a problem. She's a very capable fighter, but she's five-foot-three, and we needed an imposing presence. So it's very much about casting. You can write any description of a character that you want, but what is on the page is meaningless if you don't embody it in the physical character."

"We were looking for someone with an incredible physical presence," details Cooper, "and it's very rare to find an actor who has that physical presence who can also act. Quite often the guys that have the right look are not so good with the acting part! So that's a very big challenge. The other thing is, our production schedule seems to fall in and around pilot season, so we are always competing with the networks on pilots. Even though we are traditionally a much longer running season who's offering twenty episodes on the air, people can't seem to resist the lure of being in a network pilot. So we're often competing for actors at that time of year."

The path that led to the producers hiring Jason Momoa was a long and winding one that began with Wright and Cooper giving *Stargate: Atlantis*' casting agents a description of what they were looking for. "When we saw Jason on a tape that came up from LA, we immediately said, 'Oh, that's the guy,'" says Cooper. Apparently, the producers reaction at seeing Momoa on screen, with his broad frame, brooding look and distinctive dreadlocks, was to say "OTW!" — On To Wardrobe. They had already seen enough to convince them that they had found exactly what they were looking for. "Unfortunately there are several other hurdles you then have to cross," Cooper laughs. "We had to convince the studio and the network that he was the right guy, and that's a process."

Part of that process was to get Momoa to read in an audition with Joe Flanigan, so that both the producers and the network could gauge the chemistry between the two. "They took me down to LA to read with him," Flanigan recalls, "and I met three or four guys. I thought Jason was the right guy for sure, and luckily they picked him. It was an interesting process — we could have gone so many different ways, because each person was very different. But some of the other guys were a little too similar to me. [With them], it wouldn't have been such a balance, it would have been more of a reflection." The actor laughs, "Jason, his sheer physical presence, this massive dreadlocked dude, is unmistakably *him!*"

Even with the chemistry working well between the hero and his destined sidekick, Wright and Cooper still had a way to go before Momoa was signed for *Stargate: Atlantis*.

"It took some convincing," admits Wright. "The network didn't completely understand what it was we wanted out of the character." Cooper elaborates: "You have to do test screenings. But we ended up with our first choice and, we think, the right one."

It certainly was in the eyes of star Joe Flanigan, who found the relationship he felt the character of Sheppard had hitherto been missing. "The sidekick thing is critical for a character like ours," says the actor, "and having him is the perfect dynamic, the perfect balance of the Id. Because he's pure Id! He goes for it, he crashes the door down, he wants to get in on everything. We have to control him, and I think through that process Sheppard passes down some of his hard-earned but scant wisdom," Flanigan laughs, "which is 'think first, then shoot', as opposed to 'shoot first, then think'. It's interesting."

Wright also feels that Momoa was the perfect addition to the team, bringing with him the physical presence *Stargate: Atlantis* needed. "We had this one shot recently," says Wright, laughing at the memory, "it's something of a television cliché, but a guy grabs you by the collar and throws you up against a wall. Usually that's done with an apple box and is faked. But Jason actually, in a wide shot, lifted this guy up and held him against the wall! It was very effective, and very powerful. He's huge! And a sweetheart, and a growing actor. We're really pleased with the way that went."

Above: Ronon Dex (Jason Momoa) arrived in season two to add some muscle to the proceedings.

Having dealt with the largest change for season two, and agreed that they had found the perfect dynamic to lift the show, the producers and production crew turned their attention to other aspects of the coming season. They had always intended that the second year of the team's adventures in the Pegasus Galaxy would involve slightly closer ties with Earth and SGC, so Wright and Cooper introduced the *Daedalus*, and with it another new character in the shape of its commander, Colonel Steven Caldwell.

In developing the Caldwell character, the producers were looking to solve another character dynamics issue that had arisen during season one. "One of the reasons we brought Caldwell in was to provide more of a dramatic foil for both Sheppard and Weir," Wright explains. "The network had shown an interest in having the leads butt heads a little more as a source of dramatic tension, but in science fiction I think the fans (and I'm the same way) want to see our characters working together rather than going against each other."

"We used to get some nice conflict between Daniel and O'Neill on *Stargate SG-1*," Cooper elaborates. "There was some nice banter and bickering going on between them, and I think we originally saw the Weir/Sheppard relationship as a different version of that, where Weir was the civilian with a humanitarian point of view, and Sheppard was the military guy. We were hoping to get that sort of relationship going, [but] whenever we tried it, it didn't really work. Audiences, and us, didn't respond positively to the team bickering. Maybe it was because they were on an expedition and needed to work together and have this foxhole mentality. It just didn't seem right that they were fighting with each other. So we felt we needed a bit of a foil, someone to provide the challenge, the 'sandpaper' in certain scenes, to create an adversary for Weir. On *Stargate SG-1*, Hammond was always battling the Pentagon or someone in order to support the team, and it made Hammond's character stronger. We were looking for a way to make Weir's character stronger by having to oppose a challenge, and Caldwell was the answer to that."

"It's all about the team, it seems, with our series," agrees Wright. "And so the network said, 'Well, you need *somebody* who can still fill that role.' Yet it strikes me that there have been many times when Caldwell is as much a part of the team as anybody else. We've come up with some episodes this year where Caldwell becomes that foil character, but it's interesting in that he can go back and forth. He has a mandate that is almost strictly military, and that allows us to have him play his own agenda separate from our own, but Mitch [Pileggi] is capable, as an actor, of warming up to our characters. So he seems to be able to go back and forth quite readily."

For the first season, the producers had avoided casting 'name' talent, instead creating a team from actors who were not particularly high profile in the business. Doing so had proved a complete success, and so for the show's second year, Wright and Cooper decided they could afford to stir in some names. Mitch Pileggi is best known for his role as Assistant Director Walter Skinner in *The X-Files*, and the producers were pleased when the actor agreed to take the part of Steven Caldwell. "Mitch was on a very short list of people we were hoping to get," says Cooper. "There are certain roles that you audition people for, and then there are roles that you are hoping to cast from known actors. We knew his work, and thought he would be great for the role."

Giving the crew of Atlantis limited access to Earth was a tricky proposition, and introducing Caldwell's

Below: Colonel Steven Caldwell (Mitch Pileggi) was set to stir things up for Dr Elizabeth Weir (Torri Higginson).

ship, the *Daedalus*, was the answer. "We wanted the contact to be there but we wanted it to be limited, and that was the only way," Cooper explains. "We knew immediately that we didn't want to find a bunch of ZPMs so that we could go back and forth, because we still wanted *Atlantis* to be unique from *Stargate SG-1* and also feel as though they were still isolated to a certain degree. We had opened the world up and allowed for new blood to travel back and forth, but we didn't want to spoil the uniqueness of *Stargate: Atlantis* by having it cross over too often."

The *Daedalus*, like Caldwell, created a different dynamic for *Stargate: Atlantis* in season two. Whereas in season one, the show hadn't really been a 'ship show', the writers and directors could now tell different kinds of stories. "I love it," enthuses director Martin Wood about the *Daedalus*. "It's an Earth ship, which is something we don't do very often. When you're working with Goa'uld ships, you're dealing with a shape and not being able to put a lot of stuff in it, because everything you put in it has to be alien. It's just these spartan sets. So here, when you build an Earth set, you get to put stuff in it that you know! You can fill it up."

The ability to fill the set space, Wood explains, is important for the medium in which *Stargate SG-1* and *Stargate: Atlantis* are now shot. "Truthfully, what you want is foreground," explains the director, "because we're shooting high definition television. When you're shooting HD TV, it flattens a lot out that thirty-five millimeter film doesn't, unless you start strengthening the shots by putting foreground in them. The more foreground you can get, the more three-dimensional it feels. In something like the *Daedalus*, we redesigned it to give us a different look than the *Prometheus*. We were throwing things on the walls that we could shoot around and through, things like that. I really like shooting in that ship, especially having come from shooting the *Andromeda* and Goa'uld ships where there's nothing other than big black floors and bald columns.

Above: Dr Rodney McKay (David Hewlett) saves the galaxy... yet again.

Above: The *Daedalus*, Earth's shiny new battleship, and the Atlantis crew's way home.

This is a real treat!"

Wood and the rest of *Stargate: Atlantis'* directors were in for another treat of the ship kind later in the year, when the episodes 'Aurora' and then 'Inferno' introduced another new kind of ship — this time an Ancient war ship. But with the new sets came another set of problems for the production to overcome. "What's funny about that was, when I first saw the design on paper I said, 'I don't think we have enough ship there for us to do this,'" Wood laughs, "and they said, 'Well, that's as much money as we've got!' So what we did was redesign the ship without it costing any more by taking the dais that has the captain's chair on it and moving it way into the middle of the studio, and bringing in a couple of the little 'pianos' we had for 'Trinity'. We put people standing at them and said, 'It's a glass cockpit!' The whole thing is glass, so we're not expected to look up or around in it. When we look towards it, it's a visual effect. But how often do you do that? Unless you're looking specifically at something out of a window, you don't necessarily need to look at the front of the ship.

"A couple of times when you watch 'Aurora', there's a shot where Sheppard climbs down a ladder and he looks up a big long corridor, and you see the front of the ship. You just see a star field out there with these big stanchions that were actually part of a completely different set that I stole and put into this set as struts keeping the space out of the cockpit. That's all [physical]. That's a star field with a bunch of people standing in front of it, and these struts, and it looks like the glass front of the *Aurora* and now the *Orion*. And what's funny is, when you look back deep into the set from the cockpit, you look all the way to the back and you can actually see the stairs that are in the 'Blade' set, but they don't look like it. The whole thing about the television is you usually don't have

[big] sets, but we have nine studios working right now! And with nine *big* studios, you can actually give yourself long hallways and long ships."

Wood's ingenuity and expertise at shooting *Stargate: Atlantis'* standing sets in a multitude of different ways helped the show look fresh throughout its second year. Combined with the new cast line-up, a great new story for an existing character, and a whole slew of fabulous plotlines, *Stargate: Atlantis* succeeded in producing another twenty stunning episodes of science fiction television — and ensured that there was plenty more to look forward to in the future.

"You do go in with certain intentions," explains Robert Cooper. "For example, we originally hoped that the Weir/Sheppard relationship would be the Jackson/O'Neill relationship but in reverse, with the civilian being in charge of the military man. But as you have probably seen, that relationship has evolved very differently. In fact, Sheppard and Weir don't clash much at all, and the conflict we envisioned between them doesn't seem to work when we try. Part of this is because Weir is not on the team, and part of it is because of the tone of *Atlantis*. People seem to want to see our heroes fighting the Wraith, not each other. For some reason it just seems more petty on *Stargate: Atlantis* — maybe because it's an expedition and they are so far from home. They only have each other, and must stick together. Plus, the more amusingly abrasive dynamic between McKay and just about everyone else evolved and gave us the edge that the Daniel/Jack relationship was giving us in *Stargate SG-1*. We start with certain ideas, and at some point the actors, the characters and the series take on a life of their own." Å

Below: The *Stargate: Atlantis* team discusses strategies against the Wraith.

THE EPISODES

"You know, you may be able to make him look like a human, talk like a human — but he's still a Wraith. Nothing you do will ever change that." — *Dex*

SEASON 2 REGULAR CAST:

Joe Flanigan (Lieutenant Colonel John Sheppard)

Torri Higginson (Dr Elizabeth Weir)

David Hewlett (Dr Rodney McKay)

Paul McGillion (Dr Carson Beckett)

Rachel Luttrell (Teyla Emmagan)

Jason Momoa (Ronon Dex)

THE SIEGE (III)

WRITTEN BY: Martin Gero
DIRECTED BY: Martin Wood

GUEST CAST: Ellie Harvie (Dr Lindsey Novak), Clayton Landey (Colonel Dillon Everett), David Nykl (Dr Radek Zelenka), Mitch Pileggi (Colonel Steven Caldwell)

Sheppard's suicide mission is curtailed by Colonel Steven Caldwell of the *Daedalus* — which arrives in time to save the major as the nuke destroys the hive. The *Daedalus* beams the awaited ZPM to Atlantis, and as McKay tries to get the device working, Caldwell and Sheppard find a way to destroy the final Wraith hive. They use the ship's Asgard transporter to transfer a nuke directly inside the hive. The plan works, but the last remaining Wraith darts launch a final, coordinated attack on Atlantis. McKay powers up the shield, protecting Atlantis from aerial attack, though there are still Wraith in the city. Lieutenant Ford is discovered floating in the water around Atlantis, still connected to the Wraith that died whilst feeding on him. Ford has been kept alive by an enzyme that the Wraith injects into its victim to strengthen it while it's being fed on. Ford, though consequently physically stronger, is now dependent on the enzyme to survive. Meanwhile, McKay and Zelenka discover twelve more Hive ships on course for Atlantis. The *Daedalus* destroys two before the Wraith find a way of blocking the Asgard beam. On Atlantis, a now alert Ford's new brain chemistry makes him volatile. He attacks Beckett, and later steals the remaining enzyme. The Wraith begin to bombard the city again, and the Atlantis crew's only choice is to make the Wraith believe the city has been destroyed, using a puddle-jumper cloak to hide it from view and faking a self-destruct as the cloak goes online. Teyla connects to the Wraith to perfect the ruse and the plan works — the Wraith leave. Atlantis has been saved, but at the cost of many individuals — including Lieutenant Ford, who steals a puddle-jumper and escapes from Atlantis into the Pegasus Galaxy, alone.

WEIR: We're still here, that's our 'status'...
SHEPPARD: Don't scare me like that.

Launching into a new season of television episodes creates a whole slew of pressures for the producers, writers, directors and cast. With 'The Siege III', *Stargate: Atlantis* leapt straight back into the middle of a story that had started almost an entire year previously.

"Ending with a two-parter is one thing," says executive producer Brad Wright, "but that was actually a five-episode arc that went back to [season one's] 'The Brotherhood'. The funny thing about 'The Siege' and 'Siege II' is that the ending — the Wraith coming and us defeating them — was in fact how I originally saw the pilot. For a very brief time in *Stargate: Atlantis*' life, it was [even] going to be the movie. And

Opposite: Sheppard considers his limited options.

of course *that* pitch wasn't setting up a television series, it had to stand alone. At the end of the rescue, the Wraith have chased us back to Atlantis and we had to figure out how to get our ZPM running so that we could get the shield up to survive the Wraith onslaught. That was supposedly the climax of the first movie idea that we had for *Stargate: Atlantis*. So we knew, going into season one, that that was going to be the climatic cliffhanger at the end of the season, but we wanted to build up to it even more, and that's how 'Siege I' was born. It really didn't even have to be called 'Siege I'," Wright laughs. "It was more a story about the satellite than it was about the siege."

The fact that the story ran over so many episodes also gave director Martin Wood pause for thought when he began to consider how to open the season. "The thing about 'Siege III' was it has to be bigger than 'Siege II'," explains the director, "and 'Siege II' was *huge*. And my feeling was, I needed to make it bigger and it can't be a let down. Everybody expects the second part of the two-parter to be bigger because the first part is just set-up. So I treated the first two parts [of 'The Siege'] as set-up for the third part. Because you don't usually do three parts, that was easier to do. I could sit there, look at it and go, 'Okay, I've got to make bigger explosions, I've got to wreck more stuff, I've got to shoot more ammo — it just has to be *bigger*.' And it was!"

The episode also revealed the fate of Lieutenant Ford, and introduced the audience to his new look. For actor Rainbow Sun Francks, that meant undergoing prosthetic make-up to simulate the aging effect, and also dealing with Ford's disfigured eye. "The eyepiece is giant," says Francks with a rueful laugh. "It's like sticking a £2 coin in your eye. They have to fold it and then it expands on my eye. It's really difficult

MISSION ⊕ DEBRIEF
SGC

Wraith Enzyme

Ford's transformation from an energetic young lieutenant into an unbalanced 'super-powered' but substance-dependent soldier was a shocking example of Wraith power, even in its misuse. The cause was an overdose of an enzyme that has evolved over millennia as part of the Wraith's feeding methods. As a Wraith feeds on its prey, extracting the human's life-force, the victim's body rapidly weakens to the point of death. Since a Wraith cannot feed on a human once it is dead, Wraith physiology has developed a way of keeping its prey alive for an extended period while feeding continues. To do this, the Wraith's feeding tubes inject the prey with the enzyme, designed to artificially strengthen the victim and allowing the predator to feed at leisure. In Ford's case, the death of the Wraith during this feeding process provoked an unexpected side effect – a massive dose of the enzyme stayed in his system, and he himself survived. Along with giving Ford a strength many times that of a normal human, his body and brain chemistry had also been irrevocably altered. Though it is possible to dose oneself with the enzyme, thereby achieving an enhanced level of strength and agility, it is not recommended.

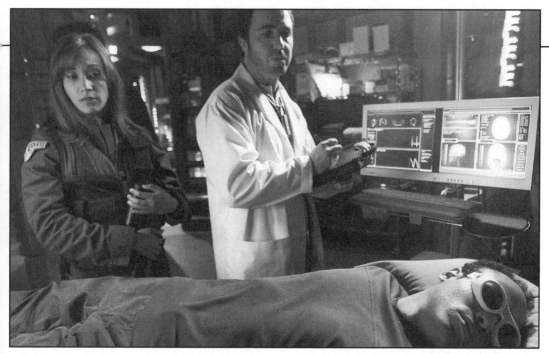

Above: The team watch anxiously over their colleague, Ford.

to get in. I think twenty-two-millimeters is the biggest [lens] the human eye can handle, and it's one less that that. When they scanned my eye, they were like, 'Oh, you have a perfect eye for this, we're going to go huge.' Most actors take it in and out throughout the day, but I found that was much more of a strain on my eye than just leaving it in and keeping it lubricated. So I left it in for the whole time, which was usually upwards of sixteen hours a day. It's hard when you're doing stunts. Your depth perception is definitely impaired."

FORD: You're all afraid of me.
BECKETT: Look at what you're doing — we have good reason to be.

The finished episode was a triumph of action and visual effects, opening the season with a classic *Stargate: Atlantis* episode. "It was *so* big," laughs Martin Wood, "and I felt that it did justice to Rainbow. It was one where you look at it and go, 'That's a good season opener, I'm happy with that!'"

"I was very happy with 'Siege III', although it might be the last three-parter I do," admits Wright. "It's very difficult to sustain a storyline for that long. Of the three, the last part is my favorite. It's got some great sequences in it that I enjoyed participating in making. It was on TV the other night and I watched twenty minutes of it — which, considering I've probably seen it six hundred times, bodes well for how much I liked the episode!" Å

THE INTRUDER

WRITTEN BY: Joseph Mallozzi & Paul Mullie

DIRECTED BY: Peter DeLuise

GUEST CAST: Beau Bridges (Major General Hank Landry), Garwin San∘ford (Simon Wallis), Lucia Walters (Lara, Ford's cousin), David Nykl (Dr Radek Zelenka), Mitch Pileggi (Colonel Steven Caldwell), Michael Boisvert (Bridge Lieutenant), Trevor Devall (voice of Hermiod)

The Atlantis crew are returning to the Pegasus Galaxy aboard the *Daedalus*, having been taken to Earth for a debrief. During the trip, a scientist called Monroe is killed in what looks like an accident. Evidence soon shows that it may have been sabotage, and when another scientist dies during the investigation, it becomes clear that something is very wrong. An intelligent Wraith program has taken control of the *Daedalus*, and sends a distress call to any nearby hive ships. With ship personnel locked out, McKay suggests a full system shut down to regain control. Sheppard uses an F-302 to physically disable the transmitter, but the program takes control of the fighter. McKay manages to retrieve Sheppard, but the fighter is lost. The shut down fails, and the program takes the *Daedalus* towards the radiation of a local star, which will kill the crew but keep the ship intact. McKay realizes that the program survived in a berthed F-302. Removing the memory chips from the fighters before another shut down should solve the problem. Asgard engineer Hermiod uses the transporter to get McKay and Sheppard to the F-302 bay, but the program opens the bay doors. Hermiod raises the shield to retain atmosphere and Sheppard and McKay manage to extract the memory chips, but have to take shelter in a fighter when Hermiod loses control. A second shutdown fails again. The program is still alive — in the lost F-302. Sheppard launches their own fighter, shooting down the affected ship. A third shutdown finally returns the *Daedalus* controls to the crew.

CALDWELL: I've got a job to do, Doctor.
WEIR: But not the one you wanted.

Having seen their heroes saved from the terrors of the Wraith in 'The Siege III', viewers tuned in a week later to discover that enough time had passed for the crew to have returned home and be on their way back to the Pegasus Galaxy once more — aboard Earth's brand new space vessel, the *Daedalus*. For Brad Wright, telling the story of what had happened in the wake of the city's salvation in this fashion avoided slowing down the pace of the season so early into its run. "We were afraid of just doing what you would call a 'housekeeping' episode," he explains, "which is, 'Well, we have to go back to Earth and we have to do this and we have to do that,' and going through the motions of that story as episode two of the season. We also wanted to show off our shiny new ship, and so the structure of flashing back [showed] the key

Classified Information

Michael Boisvert, who played the *Daedalus* Bridge Lieutenant in this episode, had previously appeared in *Young Blades* ∘ a series which also filmed in Vancouver, and whose sets were taken over by both *Stargate SG∘1* and *Stargate: Atlantis*.

Opposite: Caldwell — friend or foe?

THE INTRUDER

Above: McKay and Weir struggle with 'The Intruder'.

elements of what they needed to do on Earth without laboring it — just simply, what were the important beats?"

The introduction of the *Daedalus* became of great importance for director Peter DeLuise, who discovered that it wouldn't be as easy as it could be to integrate this new piece of hardware into *Stargate: Atlantis*. "Not only did we have a new cast member [Mitch Pileggi as Colonel Caldwell], but we had to establish early on in the season that it was his ship," DeLuise explains. "The *Daedalus* is the new and improved version of the *Prometheus*. It's a whole different class of ship, different on the outside. It's asymmetrical, and by that I mean it has a flight tower on one side and not on the other — much like an aircraft carrier would have — which is why it was designed that way. The average watcher wouldn't think that was a very big deal. But when you have an asymmetrical ship, that means you can't just take the footage of that ship and flip it so that it looks like it's going left or right. It's no longer valid to flip the film because the tower moves from one side of the ship to the other. I said, 'Hey I think we need to take a look at this because it might cost us extra money to render more footage and that money could possibly be better spent elsewhere.' But Brad Wright wanted that aircraft carrier look, so he stuck to that. That's a major quality control decision and I thought it was quite brave. That was a big deal to me, because they were going to end up spending a lot more money based on that decision."

To follow through with the design decision, and to add a little more originality to the uniforms that would be seen aboard the *Daedalus*, DeLuise asked for the crew to look like a slightly different branch of Earth military. Whereas the SGC military teams had mainly been made up of marines and air force personnel, the *Daedalus* was to look more like a navy-crewed ship. "We tried to institute what they do in the navy; with the aircraft carriers having the color-coded crew uniforms. That was just me thinking we don't see enough variety. I felt we needed some more differentiation between [air force] F-302 pilots and *Daedalus* crew members."

SHEPPARD: You did great back there, Rodney. Want to take the stick?
McKAY: Really?
SHEPPARD: No.

'Intruder' also had the job of fleshing out the newly-arrived character of Colonel Steven Caldwell, who had been seen briefly in 'The Siege III' but would now become a more integral part of life in Atlantis. For actor Mitch Pileggi, he not only had to step into a show running into its second season, but also had to get to grips with the realities of working in science fiction television — acting to green screens and issuing commands to a space ship crew, including a fractious alien...

"Mitch, to his credit, was not only coming in to a show where he was going to recur, but he had to be this commander of this whole new space ship system," laughs DeLuise. "It's not like you can just reach back into your own personal experience and go, 'Oh yeah, I know what it's like to be a space ship captain.' But, he does know what it's like to be a leader, and he did that incredibly well on *The X-Files*. I was pleased with him."

As director, DeLuise was also pleased with the method he developed to show the virus' movement around the ship. "There was no reference to any camera 'point of views', close ups of the security system cameras, in the script at all. To me, that was very disconcerting as a director, because there was no face of the enemy. There was no tangible, visual element saying 'This is the bad guy', it was just the ship, and stuff that was happening automatically. But by doing these shots of the cameras, I gave the 'bad guy' a face. To me, that was the difference that a director can make. And I know I'm patting myself on the back here — I didn't know how I was going to sell the story before I came up with that! If you remember the super-wide-angle lens shot, it has kind of a warpy feel to it. Sometimes it's called a 'fish-eye' lens. That lens has to be ordered ahead of time, and that's what we did. We ordered a special super-wide lens, with the intention of insinuating that the enemy is watching at all times. I was particularly proud of how that worked out." Å

RUNNER

WRITTEN BY: Robert C. Cooper
DIRECTED BY: Martin Wood

GUEST CAST: Kavan Smith (Major Lorne), Mitch Pileggi (Colonel Steven Caldwell), Jonathon Young (Parrish), Dan Payne (Reed), James Lafazanos (Wraith)

An Atlantis exploration team discovers a dead Wraith. Beckett's subsequent autopsy reveals that its enzyme sack has been removed — evidence pointing to Lieutenant Ford. Sheppard takes a team to investigate. Teyla and the colonel find tracks, but the suspect they are pursuing shoots and disables both of them. They come to as captives in a cave, held prisoner by an armed man who calls himself Ronon Dex. He has been tagged by the Wraith for sport — with his location device transmitting, the Wraith can track and hunt him. He met up with Ford when the Lieutenant shot dead his latest hunter. Meanwhile, McKay's search team finds Ford, who disables Major Lorne. Ford takes McKay to rescue Sheppard and Teyla, which he thinks will prove that his current state is better than his previous one and that the enzyme is the key to destroying the Wraith. Sheppard and Teyla break free, but Ronon is too quick for them. Sheppard suggests that Beckett could remove the tracker, and Ronon reluctantly agrees, but only if the doctor comes to him. If successful, Ronon agrees to help find Ford who, still accompanying McKay, is showing himself to be increasingly disturbed. Beckett arrives and manages to extract the device, despite Ronon refusing to take anesthetic or lie down. It's too late, however — three darts appear through the gate and Ronon disappears. Teyla, Sheppard and Beckett head for the gate while McKay tries to get away from Ford, who finds himself fighting with Ronon, who keeps his promise to Sheppard. Ford runs and is caught by a Wraith beam. The darts withdraw and Ronon returns with the crew to Atlantis, where he discovers that his planet has been obliterated by the Wraith.

CALDWELL: Lieutenant Ford is a significant threat to the safety of this base.
SHEPPARD: He's also a friend in need.

One of the earliest tasks that fell to the producers in *Stargate: Atlantis'* second season was the introduction of Ronon Dex, the show's new regular character. Executive producer Robert Cooper wrote the episode, developed the idea of a human being hunted by the Wraith, and reveals that in actual fact, the story for 'Runner' came along a lot sooner than the character of Ronon. "I had pitched that as a one-off story in season one," Cooper explains. "I wanted to do a story about the Wraith hunting humans. I was looking for a way in which we could expand on what the Wraith are,

Opposite: Sheppard, confronting Atlantis' problems head on.

who they are and what they do with their time. All we ever saw of them was that they were life-sucking aliens. Like the Goa'uld, they needed to be developed and turned into more three-dimensional characters.

"So I had pitched a story in which we do a sort of *Running Man* thing with the Wraith hunting humans. As the story developed and we started talking about bringing in a new character, I thought, 'Wouldn't it be cool if this guy we find being hunted turns out to be [our new] guy? He's so resourceful in running from the Wraith that he would make a great asset to the team.' And that's how it developed. The biggest change was the inclusion of Ford in the new dynamic, of what Ford was going to become, the crossover of the two characters. Having us chasing down Ford and then running across Ronon was the new element to the story that I had to weave in as I wrote it for season two. Otherwise, the idea of this sort of rough-around-the-edges, Tarzan-like survivor who was a Wraith killing machine was the idea that I pitched originally."

TEYLA: Ronon, you need to trust us.
DEX: I do. That's why he's here and you're alive.

The introduction of Ronon obviously had a huge impact on the show as a whole, and the rest of the existing cast.

"I thought it was lovely," says Rachel Luttrell of 'Runner'. "Jason showed up on set, and he was rather shy. We weren't sure quite what was going to happen and what we were going to get from him. But he's really such a sweet guy, and he's so funny. I call him a Great Dane puppy!"

"On the day they were shooting the first scene, before I filmed my scenes, I actually

Runners

The Atlantis team discovered a new facet to the personality of the Wraith following Sheppard and Teyla's introduction to Ronon Dex. Besides using their human 'herds' as a controlled food source, the Wraith also occasionally select individuals to provide them with sport. Apparently choosing the strongest and most resilient from the worlds they cull, the predators implant these humans with locator chips and set them free to be hunted again. Known as 'runners', these humans are free as long as they can evade or defeat every Wraith chasing them. From an anthropological standpoint, the idea that the Wraith participate in sport, evidently for the pure enjoyment of the chase, is an interesting discovery. It suggests a society not merely based on survival, but with culture (however alien it may seem to us), raising the further question of what other pastimes the Wraith have developed. Do they have their own form of art, of music?

Above: Dex — can he really fit in with the Atlantis team?

came in early," Paul McGillion recalls. "I hadn't seen him act before, so I wanted to watch the monitor and see what he was up to. I was impressed right away, because he had such great presence. I think some day Jason could certainly be a great action star. He looks dangerous, as if he can take men down. He has that authority. He's a really great character for the show because he has that presence, which we were somewhat missing. I think it really pulls all the team up."

Momoa's ability to look dangerous was what had attracted the producers to him in the first place, and 'Runner' would launch the actor into one of the biggest hand-to-hand fights the show had ever staged. It proved to be a rather daunting proposition. "I worked with BamBam [James Bamford, stunt coordinator] the moment I landed," says Momoa. "We probably had five sessions together, and it was something I'd never done before. I'd punched someone in a scene maybe, but not like this. I didn't know anything like that, and my guy is this big strong silent type."

All the training proved worth the effort, however, because the scene in which Ford and Dex go up against each other is one of the most memorable of the season, certainly in Robert Cooper's eyes. "I went into it saying that I thought we always fell short of having really cool fights on our show," says Cooper candidly. "We do great visual effects on our show, and I feel the dramatic scenes are always very good. I've always found that our fight stunts have always been good, but not great. I've never seen a really great fight on the show. I wanted to see us concentrate on making that fight indicative of the character we were introducing, and in some ways, respectful of the character that was moving on. So I wanted that fight to be as cool as it ultimately is. I think Martin [Wood], BamBam, Jason and Rainbow did a great job of making that look cool." Å

DUET

WRITTEN BY: Martin Gero

DIRECTED BY: Peter DeLuise

GUEST CAST: Jaime Ray Newman (Lieutenant Laura Cadman), Claire Rankin (Dr Kate Heightmeyer), Kavan Smith (Major Lorne), David Nykl (Dr Radek Zelenka), Brenda James (Dr Katie Brown)

During a survey mission to a world devastated by the Wraith, McKay and Lieutenant Cadman are captured by a Wraith dart's transport beam. After destroying it, the scientists in Atlantis manage to re-materialize McKay. It is feared that Cadman is lost — until it becomes apparent that, in fact, the young woman's consciousness is trapped inside McKay's mind, alongside his own. Meanwhile, Ronon is still in Atlantis, and is happy to share his fighting skills with the officers from Earth. Sheppard is so impressed that he wants Ronon to join the team, though Weir is not so sure. McKay attempts to get on with life with Cadman in his head. The two enter something of a power struggle, with Cadman discovering that she can take over McKay's body at certain times — including in the middle of a date the doctor had arranged with a colleague. Zelenka and McKay continue to look for a way to extract Cadman from McKay's brain pattern, without success. Eventually, though, it becomes apparent that the problem is a pressing one. The struggle that Cadman's presence has to put up in order to remain conscious in McKay's brain is causing damage to both of them. One of them needs to let go completely if either is to survive. Despite suffering from seizures, McKay comes up with a solution — a last ditch attempt to separate Cadman from his consciousness. His plan is to use a crystal from the Stargate and integrate it into the Wraith system. It's dangerous and they don't have time to test it properly, but it's worth a shot. Cadman, understanding that neither may survive, takes the opportunity to kiss Dr Beckett — much to McKay's horror. It does work, and both are restored to normal... but perhaps knowing a bit too much about each other!

CADMAN: Maybe this is a good thing! I could teach you a thing or two about the opposite sex, Rodney — Lord knows you need it!

McKAY: This is hell. This is my own personal hell.

Like many episodes of *Stargate SG-1* and *Stargate: Atlantis*, 'Duet' originally started life as the idea for a very different episode. "'Duet' came from a serious idea that was originally posed by Joe Mallozzi," executive producer Brad Wright recalls, "which was of someone being beamed into a Wraith dart and sort of becoming *The Fly*, a combination of elements. But we wanted to do that with 'Conversion'! So rather than

Opposite: Dr Carson Beckett (Paul McGillion) fights to save the lives of his colleagues.

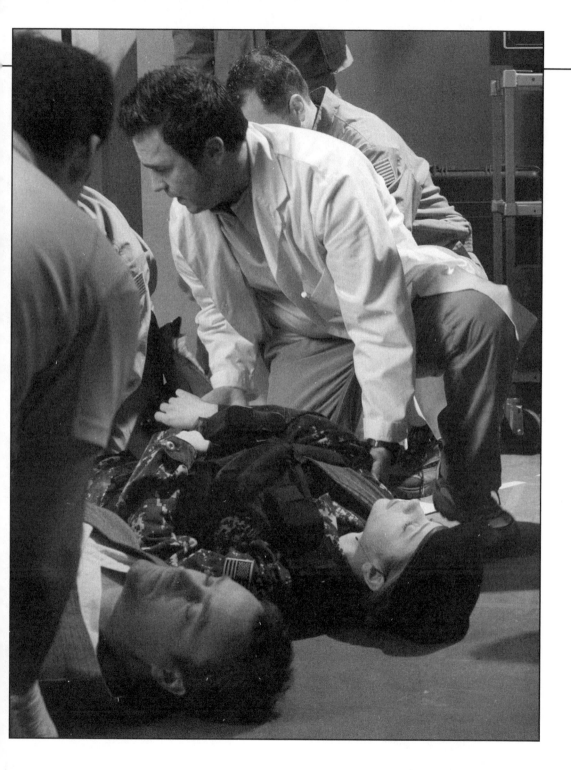

DUET

Above: Teyla Emmagan (Rachel Luttrell) tries to help Ronon adjust to life in Atlantis.

pick one of the two, Robert [Cooper] pitched, 'Well, why don't you say that McKay is beamed up with a woman?' We all immediately went 'Oh!' The humor potential of that was enormous. Of course we followed the plot all the way, and realized that there is a science fiction rationale for doing that kind of story."

"There are definitely two stand out ones for McKay having fun this year, and one of them is 'Duet'," says David Hewlett, who really got to exercise his acting muscles in a big way with this episode. "It's so funny, because I think I prefer being at work. They have so many cool things for me to do! This year it's just been endless. Brad Wright came up to me after about the second or third week [of filming] and said, 'Oh, I'm really sorry.' And I'm like, 'What? What are you sorry about?' and I was thinking, 'Oh God, I'm fired.' And he says, 'Oh, you haven't read the next episode?' And it was back to back-chatty McKay!"

Although focusing on McKay having to share his mind and body with Lieutenant Cadman, the episode also featured some character-building moments for other members of the Atlantis team, particularly Paul McGillion's Dr Carson Beckett. In fact, the episode features one of his favorite scenes in season two. "There's a really lovely scene in the start of 'Duet', where this Wraith dart almost crashes into me," recalls McGillion. "I pull my gun out and I'm not sure what to do with it. So the better part of me lowers the gun and tries to help the Wraith to a certain degree. I know a lot of people were thinking, 'What's he doing?' But he has such empathy for any creature in distress, and I think his kindness is a really lovely quality. The writers always keep that in mind and I love that — it gives him this really nice sensibility. So I really appreciate that being written in there. Of course, then Sheppard shoots the Wraith so it puts him in the situation [of thinking], 'What the hell are you doing?' He really wants to help someone but at the same time he's got to know when to stop. He probably learnt some lessons from Sheppard: 'This is our enemy. If you're coming off-world you're going to have to be prepared to fight.'"

Later on in the episode McGillion also got to display other very popular aspects of his character, as Beckett found himself struggling to understand his friend's peculiar — and hilarious — behavior. "David and I really understand each other's comic timing, so there wasn't a lot of discussion about it," the actor recalls about preparing to film his scenes. "I'm the straight guy. I like that position sometimes because you're really just listening. Good acting is about good listening, and it was such a fun opportunity to be able to play that. I think in a lot of ways in that episode Beckett is the audience's eyes. He's like, 'What exactly is going on here? I can't quite figure it out.' David did a superb job, and Peter DeLuise directed that. He's got such an interesting comedic eye as well, so it was a lot of fun to play. It was a blast!"

SHEPPARD: Did you get a chance to talk to Ronon?
WEIR: Yes, I did. Chatty fellow, isn't he?

"That was a tour de force for David Hewlett," agrees DeLuise. "You don't just write an episode like this for anybody. You have to have the confidence they can pull it off, or you don't have an episode. So this was a tremendous vote of confidence in his ability, much like [*Stargate SG-1* season seven episodes] 'Grace' was a tremendous vote of confidence for Amanda Tapping or 'Lifeboat' was in Michael Shanks. Those episodes are acknowledgements by the writing staff that they have complete confidence in that actor pulling off that episode. Otherwise, they wouldn't dare just trust the actor to be able to act this out. They would put in a whole bunch of fancy explosions and space ship stuff!"

The director also recalls that it was the actor's own choice to adopt certain mannerisms that would make it clear to the audience who was in control even when he was not speaking. "It was David's idea to actually talk to [Jaime Ray Newman], who was playing the character stuck in his mind. He adopted her nuances, her American pronunciation of words, and the speed at which she spoke because it was different from his own. He did that really well." Å

CONDEMNED

STORY BY: Sean Carley
WRITTEN BY: Carl Binder
DIRECTED BY: Peter DeLuise

GUEST CAST: Darcy Belsher (Eldon), Christian Bocher (Torrell), Alan C. Peterson (Magistrate), Kavan Smith (Major Lorne), Kyla Anderson (Marin), James Lafazanos (Male Wraith), Chuck Campbell (Technician)

A routine mission in the puddle-jumper takes Sheppard and his team to a planet where they are attacked with primitive weapons. They attempt to escape, but are saved by the arrival of an alien vessel, which then escorts them to the mainland. The planet is called Ellisia, and the island on which the Stargate stands is a penal colony. The Magistrate of Ellisia, a very advanced society, claims that the Wraith do not bother them, choosing to feed only on the prisoners from the colony, whose inhabitants are the most violent of Ellisia's criminals. Sheppard is suspicious, but McKay is curious about a mineral on the planet that may provide a power source. Weir is interested in starting negotiations, and will take over herself once the team return to Atlantis. However, as the jumper approaches the gate, it is shot down by the prisoners and crashes on the island. Taken prisoner, the team discovers that the Magistrate's claim that only the worst prisoners are housed on the island may be false. The prisoners intend to escape using the puddle-jumper, and force McKay to fix it. Weir arrives on the mainland with Lorne, concerned when the team fails to appear. McKay realizes that he can't fix the ship, but when one of the prisoners offers to free them if they take him along, he decides to try and activate the DHD so that they can leave on foot. However, before they can escape, the gate activates and a Wraith dart emerges, heading for the mainland. The Magistrate is in fact bargaining with the Wraith to leave his people alone. Weir is warned by a dissenter that the Magistrate is not interested in finding their people, only in keeping the island population well stocked. Rescinding their agreement, Weir and Lorne prepare to leave as, on the island, Sheppard, Ronon and Teyla try to keep the prisoners at bay so that McKay can finish. A Wraith cruiser arrives to feed, but McKay launches a drone to disable it, alerting Weir's jumper to their presence. Dialing the gate to the Alpha site, they let the prisoners go before redialing Atlantis and escaping on foot while the jumper flies overhead. Other cruisers, robbed of their meal, head for the mainland.

McKAY: There's no sign of any settlements, at least nothing recent.
DEX: Apart from the smoke from that campfire.

Opposite: A rare trip off world spells trouble for Dr Weir.

'Condemned' was an unusual episode of *Stargate: Atlantis*, in that the initial idea had been pitched by a freelancer, Sean Carley, rather than originating with one of the show's in-house staff. "Brad and Robert invited him in and he came and pitched,"

explains Carl Binder, who would eventually go on to write the teleplay. "He pitched an idea that was actually really good, but the problem right from the start was that it had two moral dilemmas. Originally it was pitched that these people would clone their worst criminals and put them on this island as a sacrifice to the Wraith, and the Wraith would leave the rest of them alone." For the *Stargate: Atlantis* producers, this premise seemed a little unnecessarily complicated. "Either you clone people as sacrifices to the Wraith, which is its own moral dilemma, or you use your prisoners as sacrifices to the Wraith, which is another moral dilemma. The two together kind of muddied it. As a result they decided to give the script to me. So we stripped away the clone element and just had the penal colony on this island, which I thought was very interesting. I love the episodes that deal with these moral quandaries."

One element of the original pitch that remained firmly in Binder's script through to the finished product was the explanation for why the Wraith have retained their mouth as a facial feature, despite not needing it to feed with. "Robert and Brad had been saying that we want to start to get to know the Wraith a little bit more this year," explains Binder. "One of the reasons that they approved and bought this pitch was because of that scene. It was in the original pitch that the leader of this civilization had made a deal with the Wraith in order to leave them alone, as long as they provided them with food. So there was always going to be this scene — it wasn't originally a dinner scene [as it is in the finished version], it was a scene where we sit down and have a discussion with this Wraith. They've evolved to the point where they are completely sustained by feeding on humans. Feeding by mouth is a leftover remnant of having started as humans, but it doesn't actually sustain them. It's more a pastime that they can enjoy. The other thing that we learn in that scene, too, is that the Wraith are not a total collective being. There is some individuality to them, which sets up what leads to the Wraith civil war."

DEX: Is that an order, Sheppard?
SHEPPARD: I am beat up, tied up, and couldn't order a pizza right now if I wanted to. But if you need it to be, yeah... it's an order.

The episode also gave the show's most recent star, Jason Momoa, space to evolve the character of Ronon Dex, particularly where his relationships with the rest of Sheppard's team were concerned. One early scene (from which page 38's quote is derived) allowed Dex to go head to head with Rodney McKay, something that the actor particularly relished. "Our relationship is great, because we're constantly putting each other down, but we also respect each other," says Momoa of Dex the warrior and McKay the scientific genius. "I don't think the way he thinks, he doesn't think the way I think, but there's a nice little banter between them. It's great to do."

For director Peter DeLuise, 'Condemned' marked his second experience of working with Momoa. From a directorial point of view, he explains, having Dex provided a marked difference to how the team had been shot the previous year. "Jason's big thing is that he's got cat-like reflexes, and he's a great fighter," explains DeLuise. "That in itself is going to be different from the way that we would shoot Ford. Jason doesn't resemble something that I recognize. The characters are more specialized [in season two]. Ronon has knowledge of how the Wraith operate, and he's an alien from that particular galaxy, so he has information and he can fight really well. There's less overlap between Ronon and Sheppard or Ronon and Teyla than there was between Ford and Sheppard. Ford and Sheppard were very similar in what they knew of the world and the way that they reacted to the world. It was important that they had somebody who was very different from the others, just visually and mentally."

For DeLuise, 'Condemned' underlined that Momoa was fulfilling the demands of his new role admirably, but behind the scenes, producer Carl Binder reveals that the writers were still finding their feet with the character. "I was writing 'Condemned' at the time that we were just starting shooting on the first couple of episodes," he explains. "Ronon didn't actually come in until the third episode, so he had just made his appearance. We were finding his voice, trying to find out who this guy is. Obviously, we knew who the character was and how he was set up, but then an actor inhabits the role, and you start realizing, 'Oh, okay, he can do this really well, but maybe he's not so great at this…' You write to their strengths, and I think that was at a time when we were still trying to get the voice of the character — this man of few words, man of action, man of vengeance, but with this great sense of honor and loyalty to him. So that was a work in progress," Binder continues with a laugh. "But I have really come to enjoy the character. I really like what the character brings to the show, because he is completely different from the others." Å

Above: Sheppard and Dex don't like the look of Ellisia's 'Condemned'.

Classified Information

Most of the costumes sported by the hapless convicts who take Sheppard and his team prisoner were originally created for the Kevin Costner movie *Waterworld*.

TRINITY

WRITTEN BY: Damian Kindler
DIRECTED BY: Martin Wood

GUEST CAST: David Nykl (Dr Radek Zelenka), Sean Campbell (Solen), Mitch Pileggi (Colonel Steven Caldwell), Christopher Gauthier (Mattas), Chuck Campbell (Technician)

Sheppard, McKay, Teyla and Ronon visit a world listed in the Atlantis database. Floating in orbit are the remains of a destroyed Wraith hive ship fleet, but no life signs are apparent. The planet is also a scene of devastation, but McKay is able to detect signs of a power source that is clearly Ancient. Exploring the ruins, the team finds an outpost that is still intact, full of masses of Ancient technology but also many bodies. McKay is convinced that the Ancients had discovered a weapon capable of destroying the Wraith, although it is still a mystery what actually killed the Ancients in the outpost. Weir gives the go-ahead for a team to investigate. Meanwhile, Ronon accompanies Teyla on a mission to a planet, Belka, where she hopes to open trade routes. While there, Ronon discovers that another survivor of his home world already trades with the Belkans. Teyla assumes that this will be good news for Ronon, but the young warrior promptly executes his former friend for treachery. McKay and Zelenka get to work on what they believe is more than an Ancient weapon — it's a power source that would far outstrip the energy output of a ZPM. They fail to get it to work properly, but McKay is confident that he can overcome their failings. Weir and Caldwell are doubtful, but Sheppard, convinced by McKay's confidence, vouches for his ability to make the device work. His trust is misplaced, however. McKay, determined to prove his genius, instead succeeds only in destroying the planet, almost taking himself, Sheppard and the *Daedalus* with it. The Ancients could not get 'Project Arcturus' to work — and neither can Rodney McKay.

SHEPPARD: Well... you're right. The Ancients couldn't make it work...
McKAY: I said *I* wanted to do all the talking.

'Trinity' offered another great shock of *Stargate: Atlantis*' second season — the revelation that the city's resident genius, Dr Rodney McKay, may not be infallible after all.

"I think the story derived from my believing that McKay is one of the central pillars of the Atlantis team," recalls the episode's writer/producer Damian Kindler, "and as such, what would happen if he was somehow out of control?" It was certainly an interesting premise to work from, since the idea of McKay not being able to fix a problem encountered by the team in the Pegasus Galaxy had never

Opposite: McKay discovers that he can't fix everything.

TRINITY

Above: Teyla tries to talk sense into her new team mate.

arisen before. He was Atlantis' cerebral hero — what Sheppard could not fix through action, McKay could invariably fix through brains.

"As we spun the story, it became obvious it was high time he screwed up," Kindler continues. "He is only human after all, and the implications of his ego running rampant had to be big. Plus, lets face it, writing McKay is one of the true joys in life! Up there with skiing fresh powder or a really great scotch — as a writer you consciously love putting words in his mouth!"

For Brad Wright, who provided the finishing re-write on the episode, 'Trinity' was an important learning curve, not just for McKay but also for the other characters around him. "When he says to Sheppard, 'I've learned from my mistake and I promise to be right from now on'… It's so important to McKay to have Sheppard's respect. And to me, the most powerful moments in those episodes are when Sheppard says, 'He asked me to trust him and so I put my life completely in his hands.' Even though he knew just how possible it was that Rodney's ego was out of control, Sheppard also has his own faith in his ability to get out of these kinds of situations. 'Trinity' is one of my favorites this season."

"I think from a character standpoint, the biggest shock to McKay and to his system [this season] is probably 'Trinity'," says actor David Hewlett, "because here's this self-professed genius getting it wrong. McKay screws up! I read that and I said to Brad, 'I don't know whether McKay doesn't like this episode or McKay doesn't like this episode!' It was kind of tough, because I was suddenly going, 'Well, what do you mean

I'm wrong?' So in hindsight, I think I love it, because [usually] McKay does some techno-babble and the problem is solved. Well, all of a sudden that no longer stands. We set that up — by the end of season one, McKay was [always] going to figure stuff out. And then season two just starts with this huge, *literal* bang and you've got McKay making these horrendous mistakes with these cataclysmic results."

SHEPPARD: Worst case scenario?
McKAY: You tear a hole in the fabric of the universe. Which is much less likely to happen than the Nobel prize... the risks are nothing compared to the potential benefits. Elizabeth will listen to you. I've never asked you for this before, but I think I've earned that. Trust me.

The episode also provided a chance for viewers to get to know the character of Steven Caldwell better, though not everyone liked what they saw — namely, a military leader desperate to find a new weapon in the war against the Wraith. "Of course Caldwell was there spying!" Wright laughs. "That's Caldwell — it makes sense. It doesn't come out of nowhere. It makes complete sense that he was there observing everything, unabashedly and unapologetically. I think he truly thinks, 'Yeah, I want a weapon and a power source that will solve all our problems — of course! Why should I pretend otherwise? Altruism to the degree that Weir pushes it can be a bit much sometimes. We've had some people complain that Weir is a little too much in that direction, but that's the character, that's who she is."

'Trinity' is something of a departure in style for *Stargate: Atlantis*, since it also has a second story strand — what is known as a 'b' story. Though a traditional story style in television drama, it's a method not often employed by *Stargate: Atlantis* or *Stargate SG-1*. However, Damian Kindler used it to include some important character development for new Atlantis crew member Ronon Dex, as he and Teyla Emmagan come to an understanding during a trading mission that excludes the rest of the team. "I've messed up enough times and she's backed me up and had my back," explains Jason Momoa of the relationship between the Satedan and the Athosian, "and so I have that respect for her."

For the episode's writer, both elements came together to make a particularly memorable story, of which he is very proud to have been a part. "A lot of things [worked well]," Kindler says with a smile. "Most of them begin with the word 'David' and end with 'Hewlett'! But beyond David's brilliant performance, I loved Joe Flanigan's humor, Jason Momoa's kill scene, Rachel's passion as Teyla, and the wonderful VFX from start to finish. Martin Wood did a fantastic job of making a dense science-based story really flow. All in all, I was thrilled with it." Å

Classified Information

Trinity' was the name of Earth's first nuclear explosion test. conducted by United States scientists on July 16, 1945 at the Alamogordo Test Range in New Mexico.

INSTINCT

WRITTEN BY: Treena Handcock and Melissa R. Byer
DIRECTED BY: Andy Mikita

GUEST CAST: Jewel Staite (Ellia), John Innes (Zaddik), Stephen Dimopoulos (Goran), Tom Bates (Callup), Jeffrey Robinson (Wraith)

Sheppard's team arrive on a planet at night. It is cold and dark, and everyone appears to be indoors. Suspicious of strangers, the village leader wants them to move on, but the bartender refuses to send them out after dark. There is a creature in the forest that the leader calls a "demus" — but his description clearly resembles a Wraith. Sheppard offers their expertise in catching the Wraith, a name that the leader recognizes from times past when the village was culled, but they had never known what the Wraith looked like. He tells them that about ten years ago, a craft from the sky crashed. The villagers killed the surviving aliens, but they missed one. It's still in the forest, feeding three or four times a year. Next day, the team tracks the creature and is shocked to discover a young female Wraith named Ellia, who was a child in the crash and has been adopted by a local man, Zaddik, who hid her in an abandoned mine. He swears that she has been brought up not to feed and that he developed a serum that quells her hunger. There must be another Wraith out there. Beckett is very interested to hear this, since Ellia may hold the key to his latest research — a retrovirus designed to revert the Wraith to human form. With a sample of her blood, he might be able to perfect it. Meanwhile, proof comes that there is another Wraith in the form of another death when Ellia was in their company. However, it soon becomes clear that Ellia has been hiding the truth. Her father's serum has not quelled her hunger — she still has to feed even though she detests it. In desperation, she steals Beckett's unfinished retrovirus and injects herself with it. Instead of turning her into a human, however, it brings out the Iratus bug DNA. Crazed, she saves McKay by killing the other Wraith, but kills Zaddik when he tries to calm her. Still on the run, she attacks Sheppard, biting him until Ronon shoots and kills her, bringing her tragic life to an end.

SHEPPARD: So it's a teenage thing? Pimples, rebellion, life-sucking?
BECKETT: Something like that. The question is, what causes it? If it's due to some chemical deficiency like a diabetic's inability to process sugar, then it's possible it may be addressed with some sort of drug.

Opposite: Ellia (Jewel Staite) confronts her uncomfortable past and future.

'Instinct' would put *Stargate: Atlantis* on its darkest path yet, and set the course for the rest of the season. Written by a team of two freelancers, the story showed the

possibility of a different side to the Wraith and forced the team to consider that the Pegasus Galaxy's worst predator may have a softer side — or some of them, at least.

"When I started to read it, before I had completed it, my gut instinct was, 'No, no, no, no. Teyla would be the first to draw her weapon. Teyla would be the first to resist this,'" says Rachel Luttrell, of her initial reaction to the script for 'Instinct'. But she goes on, "as I started to read it, it really did make sense to me, and my visceral response to the script was something that I actually put into the shooting [at] the beginning. Because in the beginning, she does draw her weapon and she is incredibly suspicious, but she allows herself to be open to it, and responsive."

Indeed, as a theme that would later echo again in 'Michael', Teyla's ability to show sympathy meant she exhibited one of the more measured reactions to their discovery of Ellia. "It was a very interesting shift," agrees Luttrell. "She was very, very gentle with that little Wraith girl. She was the first person to embrace that whole situation, and it was very interesting who she is and her capacity to change and her capacity for growth."

The episode also introduced Beckett's new invention — an experimental serum designed to neutralize the Iratus bug DNA in Wraith, returning them to a completely human state. For Paul McGillion, it meant a meaty storyline that he was only too eager to get his acting teeth into. "That was a great episode and I really enjoyed working with Andy [Mikita]," says the actor. "I thought the humanity in the relationship with Ellia in 'Instinct' was just really interesting, the way it was played and the way it was written. You really felt for her as a character, and Jewel did a great job playing her. You don't know if we're delving into something we shouldn't be doing or not, and that

MISSION (Å) DEBRIEF

SGC

Retrovirus

Following the discovery of the Wraith's provenance by the Atlantis team, Dr Beckett began conducting his own experiments in separating the Iratus bug DNA from strands that remained human. Doing so, he hoped, would neutralize the aspects of the being that made it Wraith, thereby perhaps providing the means to end the constant state of oppression of humans through fear by Wraith in the Pegasus Galaxy. Beckett had hoped that the discovery of Ellia could provide him with the missing parts of his research that would lead to a sample ready to test. Unfortunately, Ellia chose to take the earliest incarnation of the serum, which had the reverse of the effect than was desired. Instead of neutralizing the bug DNA, the retrovirus erased the human DNA, forcing Ellia into a pre-evolved Wraith state. Continuing his research despite this event, he used what he had learned from the girl's tragic demise and Sheppard's subsequent infection to produce a second serum to a high enough standard to risk testing on a live subject — a captured Wraith known as Michael. Though the test can technically be considered a success, Michael still retained a sense that he was something 'other', an outcast. Subsequent to his escape, the Wraith returned with the idea of using the retrovirus as a weapon. An idea that troubled Beckett's healer sensibilities.

makes for an interesting dilemma for Beckett. We're doing this to fight a villain, but if the villain comes essentially from humanity, it's like, what exactly are we doing?"

TEYLA: Was that really necessary?
DEX: You can dress her up and teach her table manners, but that's not going to change who she is.

The episode was directed by Andy Mikita, who is also full of praise for guest star Jewel Staite. "Jewel, of course, is part of the *Firefly* franchise, so it was pretty exciting having her come in and auditioning for the role," he says, "and to accept the role, given that she was going to be completely unrecognizable because she was going to be completely in make-up, which she had never worn before. So she took a chance herself. It's a pretty uncomfortable position for an actor to be in to have to wear prosthetic make-up for hours on end. The length of time it takes to put the make-up on, the discomfort of actually having to wear it and then the time taking it off again — the days were long for her, and she'd never experienced that before. But I think she did a great job, and she was great to work with and a wonderful actor, and I thought she hit it out of the park. 'Instinct' would not have been nearly as good had we not had Jewel. And she seemed to enjoy herself."

Mikita also appreciate the detail that the episode's director of photography produced for filming. "Michael Blundell, had talked about trying to create a look for it — a sort of *Sleepy Hollow* feel, with lots of heavy moss and smoke. The scene where they first come into the bar is sort of an homage to *An American Werewolf in London*, where the two guys go into the bar in a little town. We had a real theme to it, which was great. I enjoyed 'Instinct' and one of the great reasons was that we shot in the forest, which was great fun — I love shooting outside." Å

CONVERSION

STORY BY: Robert C. Cooper & Martin Gero
TELEPLAY BY: Martin Gero
DIRECTED BY: Brad Turner

GUEST CAST: Kavan Smith (Major Lorne), Mitch Pileggi (Colonel Steven Caldwell), Matthew Harrison (Scientist), Lindsay Collins (Scientist), Todd Hann (Bravo Leader), France Perras (Nurse), Andy Nez (Soldier)

Returning to Atlantis following his run in with Ellia, Sheppard is rushed to the infirmary, only to discover his wounds have miraculously healed and he seems to be in physically perfect condition. Taking a blood sample, Beckett is disturbed to discover that he has been infected with the retrovirus. They have no idea what to expect, and all they can do is monitor Sheppard's progress. Caldwell, hearing the news, returns to Atlantis ready to take over Sheppard's duties, though Weir isn't too keen. Sheppard soon starts to notice a change in his skin which becomes rapidly worse. Beckett realizes that the virus is changing his DNA, causing him to devolve swiftly. The doctor has no idea how to treat it, and he has only days to find a cure, though he feels that Iratus bug stem cells could hold the key. For that they need bug eggs, and Lorne volunteers to try and bring some back. Sheppard's personality begins to deteriorate and he confines himself to his quarters. Lorne's team finds a nest, but there's no way to get past the creatures without being attacked. Meanwhile, Caldwell assumes Sheppard's role and angers Weir by immediately making changes to the security measures on base. Sheppard's time is running out and as his transformation speeds up he tells Weir to double his security detail — he is no longer safe. Having lost two men trying to retrieve the bug eggs, Lorne scraps the mission, leaving Beckett with no options. Sheppard, completely taken over by the bug, languishes near the point of no return. Beckett realizes that Sheppard himself may be the answer. His pheromones now so closely match the Iratus bug that he will be able to walk into the nest unnoticed. Overdosing him with an inhibitor that may kill him, Beckett is able to get the colonel lucid enough to explain the plan. It is almost too late, but Sheppard completes his most important mission in time to save himself.

SHEPPARD: I thought you said you were a runner?
DEX: That's funny.

"'Conversion' was a fun one," says writer Martin Gero with a laugh. "It's funny because, when Joe [Flanigan] read 'Duet', he was like, 'When are you going to write an episode that's just for me?' And I said, 'You're the star of the show! Every episode I write that's not about David is about you!' And he said, 'I want some meat!' which I read as, 'I want to be uncomfortable like you made David uncomfortable'!"

The result was an episode that would give the lead actor his first taste of prosthetic

Opposite: Sheppard finds himself undergoing a chilling transformation.

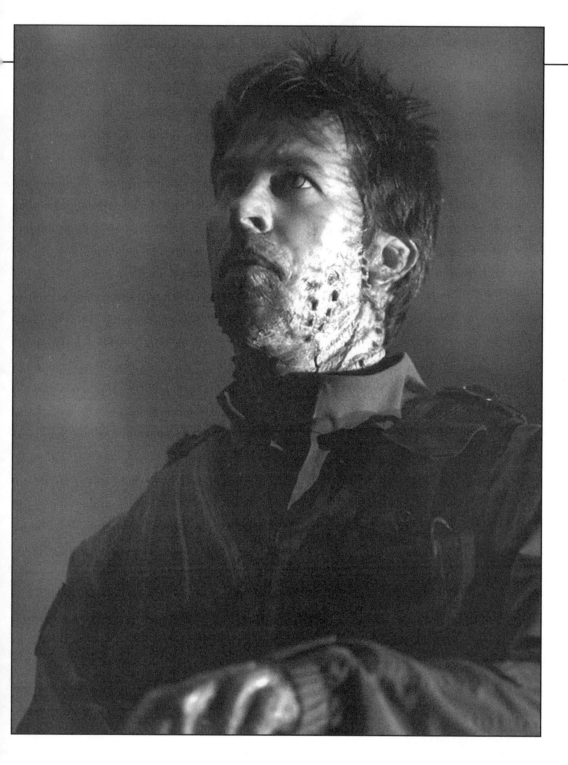

Above: The team hopes there is enough of their Sheppard left to save himself.

make-up, which Flanigan confesses was his main concern when he first read the script. "That was primarily an issue because I thought it could be really hokey if the make-up wasn't good," Flanigan explains. "But the make-up was superb. Other than that, the script was very good and very tight. It was extremely well written — Martin's one of my favorite writers."

Though the finished episode was an unqualified success, Gero is quick to confess that originally, his enthusiasm for writing the script wasn't at its zenith. "I didn't really want to write the 'Joe turns into a bug' story," he says frankly. "I thought it was kind of dumb. But like everything, you just have to sit down and think, 'Okay, what is the for-real, *cool* version of this?' I've seen this episode a thousand times on other shows and in movies — there's only nine stories in science fiction! The way you make it different is how it affects your characters. So for me, interestingly enough, I made it less about Joe turning into a bug and more about what that was doing to the rest of the team. That was really important — how his change was affecting us and how responsible we started to feel, and how powerless we started to feel. And it almost turns into a cancer metaphor — what can you do? There's a certain powerlessness when someone you love is sick and you feel like you've exhausted all your possibilities. My favorite scene in that episode is when they're all just sitting in the cafeteria at night saying, 'I can't sleep. I don't know what to do.' That's when the show really shines. Our show is about how much our characters love each other, not to sound incredibly cheesy! It is about killing the Wraith, but I think what people really latch on to is how much the team works as a team and really respects and cares for each other. And Joe's great. I think that is maybe his best performance."

Flanigan certainly got to push his character to extremes for 'Conversion', as the Iratus bug DNA began to change the 'good guy' viewers knew into someone more unpredictable — and more violent. One of the most shocking moments of the episode is his attack on Weir, in which our usually controlled hero holds his female colleague against the wall by her throat.

"Yeah, that was very dark," agrees Gero. "It's funny people always say that that's a dark scene, but I think the kiss is *really* uncomfortable. I was the most uncomfortable about the kiss, because it's violent. I really thought that maybe we had gone too far when we were cutting it together — because it's our good guy essentially forcing himself on one of our main female characters. And I think that because they have such a strong relationship, people didn't feel it — but that was an uncomfortable scene to watch."

SHEPPARD: Did Ronon shoot me?
WEIR: You had it coming.

"I was actually very excited about it," recalls Rachel Luttrell of filming the kiss scene. "I thought it was going to be a very cool scene, and ultimately I think it turned out to be. I guess one of the initial edits of it, it did look a little bit more rough," she laughs, "and I think he [Martin Gero] was very uncomfortable about that. He actually came and talked to me and said that he'd seen the edit and it looked like I was really being put upon. But the fact of the matter is, Teyla can handle herself! I think if she really didn't want to share a kiss with Sheppard, she would have been okay. I liked the ambiguity of it. Did they both enjoy it? Obviously there is a shock for both of them, and you don't really know what the undertow is, and I like that."

The scene also marked Luttrell's first ever experience of filming an on-screen kiss, and events conspired to make it particularly memorable! "My parents were visiting," laughs the actress. "It was the most bizarre thing, because I was trying to decide — do I invite them to the set? Because obviously they want to come and they want to support me, but it was that day: first of all the big fight — and when you're dealing with choreography, that's difficult enough — and then it ends with a kiss! But anyway, they came. So I think it was very difficult for Joe — he came up to me and whispered in my ear, 'Did you *have* to bring the folks?' But they were fantastic. I've got a good relationship with my parents, so it was fine. Every time we'd do a take I'd go back up and Dad would say 'Good stuff, honey, and Joe looks like a hero! Go to it!' But how hilarious that they were there [that day]. It was very bad timing! But it turned out fine, and I think it made me lighten up a little bit too because I was nervous." Å

AURORA

STORY BY: Brad Wright &
Carl Binder
TELEPLAY BY: Carl Binder
DIRECTED BY: Martin Wood

GUEST CAST: Mitch Pileggi (Colonel Steven Caldwell),
Bruce Dawson (Captain), James Lafazanos (Wraith),
Pascale Hutton (First Officer), Ryan W. Smith (Crewman)

A previously dormant Ancient warship answers an automated recall and begins its return to Atlantis. The *Daedalus* takes Sheppard's team along to investigate, and discovers a very damaged ship full of inhabited stasis pods. The crew is still alive, their minds connected to a virtual environment. McKay decides to get into an empty stasis pod to communicate with the captain, but Sheppard overrides him and connects himself. Once inside, he discovers that the ship is called the *Aurora* and her crew don't know they are in stasis. They think the war is still on, and have a vital mission to transport information about a Wraith weakness to Atlantis. They are trying to modify the hyperdrive to do so more swiftly. Sheppard realizes that Earth could benefit from whatever intelligence the captain has about the Wraith, but he can't convince the captain, and is continually blocked access to him by the first officer. The *Daedalus*, meanwhile, detects Wraith cruisers approaching, and when Teyla and Ronon discover a Wraith in a stasis pod that's clearly entered the virtual environment, Caldwell gives McKay fifteen minutes before he destroys the *Aurora* to keep it from falling into Wraith hands. McKay enters stasis himself to locate the colonel. While inside, he realizes that the whole point of the Wraith infiltrating the program is to learn how to modify the hyperdrives. Doing so will teach the Wraith how to advance their own technology — enough for them to get to Earth. McKay exits the program and disconnects the Wraith. Sheppard still hasn't left the program, trying to get the now-believing captain to release the information, but he doesn't have it. Whatever it was, it's gone. The *Aurora*'s captain uses the ship's self-destruct to destroy the approaching Wraith cruisers. The *Daedalus* escapes, and Earth is kept safe once more.

SHEPPARD: Any way to figure out what they're saying?
McKAY: Yes, of course. It's right here: "Why is the smart one having to stop and answer so many questions?"

If one of the aims of *Stargate: Atlantis'* first season was to introduce the terror of the Wraith, while its second year was determined to explore the race that had first brought Earth's attention to the Pegasus Galaxy — the Ancients.

Opposite: The Wraith spy is
revealed.

"The story was actually Brad [Wright]'s idea," says Carl Binder, who co-wrote the episode with the show's executive producer. "He pitched it to me on the phone, and

I thought, 'Oh, this is really interesting.' I loved the idea of seeing this Ancient warship. Brad's main push was that the Ancients created the Stargates, and were these incredibly brilliant people. But just like humans, you have incredibly brilliant humans and not so incredibly brilliant humans. He wanted to show that this is the crew of a ship. They aren't necessarily the ones who built and designed the ship, but they are the ones that run the ship. It was to take [the Ancients] down a few notches as far as the reverence that we have towards them, to show that there are some ordinary ones as well. So then I worked out the outline, and it was at that point that we inserted the idea that a Wraith had infiltrated the virtual reality. I came up with the idea that the Wraith took the form of a woman."

Aurora also gave the *Stargate: Atlantis* crew a chance to try something different — a completely ship-based episode, split between their shiny new toy, the *Daedalus*, and the dilapidated Ancient ship, the *Aurora* herself.

"The story of that episode," says Wright with a burst of laughter, "is that when I first saw the set, I got scared because it was so small. But Martin Wood made that tiny-looking set look like an enormous space ship *so* well! When you see the episode, you'll go, 'That's small? How could that be?' He did an excellent job. Space ships are tricky things to build, because they have gadgets and buttons and glowy things that are expensive, and to not do that makes it just look like a hallway, not like a space ship. So while there are CG elements to the set, it still looks, I think, remarkably good. Also, it existed both as the derelict and as the shiny new ship, so it was pulling double duty and had to have that look."

Besides an expert director's eye, what also assisted Martin Wood in making the

MISSION DEBRIEF

SGC

Ancient Ships

Though the current inhabitants of Atlantis, and indeed SGC before them, have spent considerable time studying Ancient technology left behind in the city and on Earth, it was only with the discovery of the *Aurora* that Earth scientists were able to examine a functioning — or at least semi-functioning — Ancient warship. Though the technology involved in such a construction is of a magnitude too large to address properly here, an interesting note can be made about the names chosen by the Ancients for their warships. The fact that the Ancients were not a warlike race out of choice but rather out of necessity may explain why their ships were called by such innocuous names as *Aurora*. Literally meaning 'the first light, or dawning, of day', and also referring to the atmospheric light phenomenon occurring over the Earth (and presumably other planets), the word 'aurora' does not conjure up the image of threat or strength that one would expect from the usual nomenclature of war. Rather, such a name echoes the Ancient's interest in enlightenment and environment.

Aurora bridge set look bigger than its actual physical size was the magic of computer art, as visual effects supervisor Mark Savela explains: "In 'Aurora', because of time and everything else, we only had space to build half a set. When we go into the virtual world, the bridge set was half a set, and we never really had the 'front' of it. That was all a 3-D set extension so that we could move the camera around and still be in that world. We could look 360 degrees and still keep in there. I think those shots really were quite seamless — I don't think you would ever say [from watching] that the set didn't exist beyond the captain's chair!"

Above: Sheppard gets up-close and personal with the crew of an Ancient vessel.

TEYLA: Are you sure you want to do this?
McKAY: I'm sure I don't.

The advantage of using computer-generated effects to expand the size of the set, Savela says, is that directors are less restricted and the writers' full vision as in the script can be realized. "With the *Aurora* bridge especially, it was supposed to be this massive, massive bridge. To build something to that scale would have been huge, so to do it this way was kind of cheaper. It certainly gave us a bigger world in there than just half of a set or only being able to shoot one way into the set. That would have really limited the directors in what they could do."

"This was my first full year on the show, and the first science fiction show that I've ever worked on," says Carl Binder, "so I was just blown away by the art department on this show, and the sets that they design. The look for this episode especially was just stunning. It was very effective, and I was very happy with it." Å

Classified Information

Bruce Dawson, who here plays the beleaguered Ancient captain, previously appeared in *Stargate SG-1*'s sixth season episode 'Forsaken'.

THE LOST BOYS

WRITTEN BY: Martin Gero
DIRECTED BY: Brad Turner

GUEST CAST: Rainbow Sun Francks (Aiden Ford).
Kavan Smith (Major Lorne). David Nykl (Dr Radek Zelenka).
Aaron Abrams (Kanayo). Paul Anthony (Jace).
James Lafazanos (Wraith). Andee Frizzell (Hive Queen)

A trading mission goes wrong when Sheppard's team are captured by Aiden Ford and a group of his followers. At his secret base on an unknown world, Ford relates how he escaped the Wraith dart and then started to gather other people willing to take the enzyme to fight the Wraith. He wants the team to take it too, convinced that it is not only safe, but a sure way of defeating the enemy. Ford has laced McKay, Teyla and Ronon's food with the enzyme. He wants Sheppard to stand witness to what it can do. Sheppard decides to play along until they can work out what to do. Ford sends the colonel and Teyla to observe one of his group's operations, while Ronon and McKay remain behind as hostages. Back on Atlantis, the search for the missing team has begun, but there is little to go on, and Zelenka tries to work out from the DHD on the first planet where the team was taken. Back with Ford, the team discovers the young man's plan — to destroy a Wraith hive ship. The former lieutenant needs Sheppard's help to execute the master part of his plan — to fly a Wraith dart they have captured inside one of the hives, with Sheppard's team and a group of Ford's followers inside the transporter beam. Sheppard plays along, believing that if he can fly them off the planet he can take the ship back to Atlantis. He attempts to convince Ford to abandon the plan and come home to Atlantis. Ford seems to be going along — but at the last moment he changes his mind and forces McKay to stay behind as a hostage. Sheppard has no choice but to go along with the original plan. The dart enters the hive easily enough, but once inside an autopilot kicks in and Sheppard loses control. He re-materializes the team, but three of Ford's men reappear in mid-air and fall to their deaths. Exiting the dart, Sheppard shoots dead two Wraith and sets off an alarm that alerts the rest of the ship. The team fight, but one by one they are captured. On Atlantis, Weir refuses to give up the search...

FORD: I know you think I'm crazy. I brought you all here to show you that you're wrong. Do I look crazy? Do I seem out of control?
McKAY: Are we speaking in relative terms, or...?

'The Lost Boys' saw the continuation of the story of Atlantis' lost lieutenant, Aiden Ford. Not seen since Sheppard's team encountered the damaged young man in 'Runner', it turned out that Ford had been keeping himself plenty busy, building his own enzyme-charged army against the Wraith. However, as recurring guest star

Opposite: Ronon and Teyla
— a formidable pair.

Above: Ford tries to make Sheppard see his point-of-view.

Rainbow Sun Francks reveals, the episode as it finally appeared on screen was very different to what had originally been discussed in early meetings.

"Along the storyline we learn that the different hive ships have different queens running their own show. We thought they were one unified mind like the Borg [in *Star Trek*], but they're not. They're doing their own thing. They're running along the same lines, but there are still separations. So what we were thinking of doing was having a group of renegade Wraith, and I actually say to them, "You guys can eat as much as you want on these planets, but only who I say you can. I'll make sure you guys are set up, but I make the rules." So originally I was going to have a gang of Wraith. And the whole time, Ford thinks he's still good. He thinks he's gathering intel for Atlantis! The whole time I was with these Wraith I would be gathering intel. And then when I see [the team], they'd be like, 'What, are you crazy?' Ford would be like, 'No, no, I'm with you guys. I'm helping.' But when I got the script, that's not what they had written, they had written this whole storyline about these guys. So I don't know if they had something different planned in the long run."

Despite the eventual route that the evolved story took, Francks enjoyed working on the episode. "I loved 'The Lost Boys'," he says. "I thought it was a fun episode to do. There were a couple of things where I think they made Ford go too far — but it's all to push the story along, and you can say that about any episode. All in all, I thought they were really well written and I had a good time."

"I thought it was one of Rainbow's better episodes, for sure," Joe Flanigan agrees. "I enjoyed that episode. Sometimes it's a tough sell when you've got young kids that are your so-called enemy. It might get as dirty as kicking sand in each other's face, type of thing. So in general, I'm skeptical about being able to do that [and in 'The Lost Boys'] we go up against a bunch of teenage kids. So I was skeptical about it, but it turned out well."

SHEPPARD: I know. Be patient.
DEX: Historically, that hasn't been a strength for me.

The episode also features some of the best fight scenes of the season, both between Ford and Ronon and also between teammates Ronon and Teyla. Actress Rachel Luttrell confesses that she was so into the fight she performed with Jason Momoa that they got a little too close… "'The Lost Boys'. Oh my goodness, that was a ball to do," she says, laughing guiltily. "Jason will never let me live this down… We did that scene over and over again, and it was great and perfect each time. We both had a lot of fun with it, because obviously we're both ramped up and it was a fun fighting scene. But the very last take of the day was where the fight starts off with me clipping him in the jaw. It was the very last take, and we'd done it so many times, and I knew that we needed another one. I pow-wowed him! I gave him a black eye! I felt so bad. It was so crazy, because I pride myself on being really determined and focused, because you have to be so careful. It goes so fast, and you really have to be deliberate in your movements, and I pride myself on that. And when I made contact… and you should have seen his face, he was so shocked!" The actress laughs again, "And that's the take they kept, because he was so shocked. His eye was turning red, and he just looked at me in total disbelief. Apparently I've got a really good punch!"

"Yeah, little punk!" Momoa exclaims in mock indignation. "She just got a little too close and clipped me. My eye turned red, and everything. The crew thought it was hilarious — 'Oooh, Jason got beat up by a *girl*!'" Å

THE HIVE

WRITTEN BY: Carl Binder
DIRECTED BY: Martin Wood

GUEST CAST: Rainbow Sun Francks (Aiden Ford),
Aaron Abrams (Kanayo), Kavan Smith (Major Lorne),
Jenn Bird (Neera), David Nykl (Dr Radek Zelenka), Mitch Pileggi
(Colonel Steven Caldwell), Andee Frizzell (Hive Queen)

Trapped on the hive, Sheppard is interrogated by the Wraith Queen, but the questioning is interrupted when the female is distracted by something — the arrival of another hive ship. At Ford's secret base, McKay tries to convince his captors that something has gone wrong, but they refuse to give him the crystals so he can dial the gate. Desperate, he decides to take more enzyme to give him the strength to overpower his guards. Sheppard and the team manage to break out of their cell and try to make their way to the dart bay where they hope to commandeer a ship with which to escape. McKay manages to return to Atlantis, but he is so high on the enzyme that he is hardly coherent. Sheppard's group pauses to rescue several Wraith victims, but in doing so they are captured again. Sheppard and Ford are incarcerated with a girl they rescued, but soon realize that she is a plant to gather information — part of a sect that worships the Wraith. In Atlantis, McKay eventually detoxes enough to explain to Weir what happened, and is able to give them the coordinates of the planet the Wraith are headed towards. If they use the *Daedalus*, they might be able to beam Sheppard and his team out of the hive. When Sheppard is brought before the Wraith Queen, he calls her bluff and says that they are in league with the other hive, which has told them how to infiltrate her ship. His life is in danger until Ford comes in firing, offering to hold back the Wraith while Sheppard escapes with the others. McKay and Lorne can't detect any of the team's life signs on either Wraith vessel, and Caldwell decides to destroy both hives before they can cull the planet and possibly report that Atlantis is still intact. Sheppard, flying a dart and scooping up Teyla and Ronon in its transporter beam, heads for the atmosphere, where he fires on the hives, making them think each is attacking the other. They are both obliterated and the dart disappears, presumed destroyed... but Sheppard's team beat Caldwell home by traveling through Atlantis' gate.

HIVE QUEEN: Where did you get the ship?
SHEPPARD: Do you mean the dart? We call them darts because they're so... pointy.

As a way to kick start the second half of the season, you can't get much better than a desperate fight for life aboard an enemy ship. Throw in a bunch of renegade soldiers and some dubious-looking young women, and it's a recipe for success. The team's eventual escape from the Wraith hive didn't run quite as smoothly as all that, though.

Opposite: Can Sheppard save his team from 'The Hive'?

As writer Carl Binder explains, producing a stunning finale to a story that you didn't begin to write is something of a challenge. "Martin [Gero] and I, our offices are side by side and we talk a lot, and we worked out the two stories ['The Lost Boys' and 'The Hive']. But still, we were writing both episodes at the same time, and that's a little bit difficult. You come out with the scripts and you think, 'Oh, okay, I've got to change this and that and we've overlapped here and there.' The idea was to make it a two-parter, but at the same time make them feel like two separate episodes that could stand on their own. If you missed 'The Lost Boys', you could still watch 'The Hive' and follow it. We felt that there was something missing in the story, and that was when Brad came up with the idea of putting the Wraith worshipper in. He had always wanted to insert that element at some point, and now was a good time to do it. That was just setting up for the future, and really filled it out."

Unusually, the episodes of the two-parter were helmed by different directors. Brad Turner, who would later depart the series to become a regular director on hit serial drama *24*, took 'The Lost Boys', while Martin Wood directed 'The Hive'. To help the continuity and make sure that everything hit the schedules, the two directors conferred on how best to present the finished episodes. "Both of us shot pieces of each other's shows," explains Wood. "Normally it would have been done as a two-parter, but in order to have Brad Turner do the number of shows we wanted him to do, we had to do it that way. So we were mixing the scripts up. It was actually very interesting swapping around like that, and I think that [our] styles are not too dissimilar. I love looking at Brad's work. He does a really good job of combining camera movement and performance."

MISSION ⊕ DEBRIEF

SGC

Wraith Acolytes

During Sheppard's time in the Wraith hive during his teams kidnap at the hands of Ford's 'task force' he experienced a new cultural phenomenon — Wraith worship. Neera, a young woman willingly used by her masters to try and manipulate Sheppard into divulging information, was later revealed to be part of a sect who worship the predators as superior beings. Though the Atlantis team had not encountered this before, the emergence of such a sub-culture in the Pegasus Galaxy is something that the anthropologists on the team and at SGC must have theorized about. Powerful beings have always been able to oppress and dominate less technologically advanced races, either through brute force or manipulation. The early population of Earth succumbed to the Goa'uld in the same way, worshipping as gods those who 'miraculously' exhibited great powers. In some cases, such worship may be a method of self-preservation. Establishing oneself as a useful and loyal servant ensures survival, at least for a time. It is possible that such worshippers have simply adapted to their circumstances the best way they could, by choosing servitude to their aggressors rather than death.

One of the most memorable aspects of 'The Hive' was McKay's frantic, drug-fuelled attempts to reach Atlantis and alert them to the team's situation. Getting the right tone for those scenes was something that the producers and both directors worked on at length, and in fact the scene in which McKay tries to get the DHD to work was re-shot, with Hewlett providing a new voiceover.

McKAY: Did you ever doubt me?
WEIR: Yes, several times.

"It was one that Brad had shot," Wood explains. "One of the mistakes that happen when you're shooting each other's shows, is that Brad didn't know where he had to go next with it. When we watched it back, Brad Wright and I both felt that McKay was too crazy. The whole scene was shot big [closer up], and he was so wired [that] he had nowhere to go once he came back into the gate room. And so the decision was made to do it over a wide shot like that instead and have him re-voice it. So that's really the reason. It was a beautiful scene, really well shot, it was just that the performance would have been too big for him [to build on]."

Actor David Hewlett thinks that the change was an appropriate one, despite enjoying filming the original footage. "We changed a few of the lines and made it a little more dreamy rather than freaked out," he explains. "I think that was wise, because the reality is when you're on this stuff of course you're flying high and enjoying yourself and thinking everything's great. I loved the wide shot, because it's much, much funnier to me, to see this little guy talking to himself in the middle of nowhere!" Å

EPIPHANY

STORY BY: Brad Wright and Joe Flanigan
TELEPLAY BY: Brad Wright
DIRECTED BY: Neil Fearnley

GUEST CAST: Chad Morgan (Teer), David McNally (Avrid), Nicole Muñoz (Hedda), Scott Miller (Pilot)

Flying over a planet, McKay spots an energy spike and the team lands to investigate. In a ridge of rock is what seems to be a doorway covered in Ancient script, emitting an energy signature. The door seems to have a cloak protecting it. Having run a peremptory test with a camera, McKay concludes it is safe and Sheppard goes in to investigate further. He is immediately gripped by the energy field, which pulls him in, causing a lot of pain. Once on the other side, he tries to contact the team but can't. Outside, McKay realizes that the playback recording they took as a test actually shows hours of footage. Sheppard has passed into a realm where time moves far more quickly — and if they can't find a way to free him very fast, he'll die of old age. Sheppard spends three days waiting for his team, thinking they have forgotten him. Eventually he heads into open country, where he encounters a man being pursued by a semi-solid creature. He fights it off and is injured. Taken to a small village where he is looked after by a woman called Teer, Sheppard learns that it is a colony of Ancient progeny who have spent their lives within the time dilation field learning to ascend. His only way out is through ascension. Stuck in the village, Sheppard encounters the monster again, and manages to fight it off a second time. As he gradually gets used to village life, he realizes that what is preventing the last of the villagers from ascending is their fear of the monster and their inability to confront it. Meanwhile, the Atlantis team decides to enter the portal and find the power source generating the field. If they can shut it down, they can get Sheppard out. Their entry awakes the beast, but the villagers finally defeat it, triggering the final element they need to ascend.

McKAY: Okay, so we tape it to the stick, extend the camera through, record for a few minutes, play the recording.
SHEPPARD: Yeah! MALP-on-a-stick!

'Epiphany' had its roots in star Joe Flanigan's personal desire to pen an episode of *Stargate: Atlantis*. Originally, the idea was to explore a little of John Sheppard's backstory, which the actor was eager to develop. Although, for various reasons, those elements of the original idea didn't quite make it into the finished episode, 'Epiphany' still managed to provide an interesting insight into the character — in particular his resourcefulness and dedication to life in Atlantis.

Opposite: What is it with Sheppard and those Ascended women?

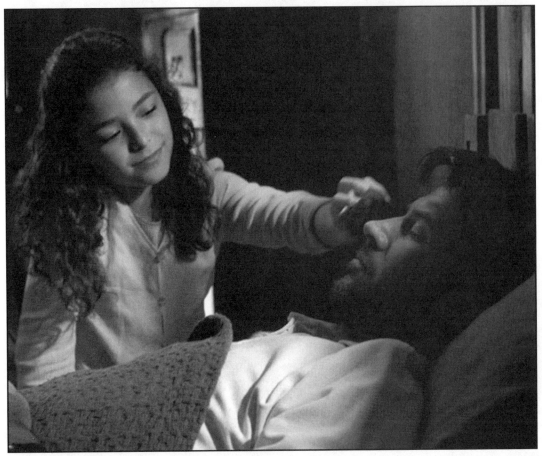

Above: Grizzly Sheppard experiences life in the country.

The original concept for the story was very different to what ended up on screen. "It was difficult to be objective when [we were] filming," Flanigan admits, "because I had ideas in my head that didn't quite come out. It changed a lot. I originally had the idea for it to be a McKay and Sheppard story, something along the lines of *The Man Who Would Be King*."

However, *Stargate SG-1* had already explored similar stories in episodes such as season one's 'The First Commandment' and season eight's 'It's Good To Be King'. As a result executive producer Brad Wright, who developed the idea alongside the show's star, suggested a different approach which succeeded in developing more of *Stargate: Atlantis*' Ancient mythology.

"It was a little bizarre, in some ways," says Flanigan of filming the first script with which he had been so closely involved in its earliest stages, "because you have an image in your head. For example, I had an image of our main antagonists — plural! They were a whole group of pterodactyl-like things that would come in, attacking from the sky, a little like *Van Helsing*, that type of thing." However, that wasn't quite how the 'beast' actually appeared on screen. "By the time we got to shooting, through visual effects changes, it became one monster in a pink outfit in a field! And it looked totally pathetic," Flanigan says with a laugh. "It was very sad to look at this thing! I was told, 'Don't worry, the pink rubber is used especially for CGI.' But it was very strange to be fighting 'Pepto-Bismol monster' out in the middle of nowhere when I was envisioning the sky darkening with a whole sea of pterodactyls! So your vision of what you wanted to do and the reality of what you end up doing — there's a major canyon between the two things. But you work with it and you work through it, and Brad said the whole monster stuff turned out really well."

SHEPPARD: I never thought I'd see any of you again. Kind of even missed you a little...
DEX: Yeah, well, it was only a couple of hours for us, so...

The episode also gave Dr Weir a chance to get out of the city of Atlantis and exercise her own area of interest: Ancient history, language and technology. This was welcomed by actress Torri Higginson, who was interested in showing a more excited, effervescent side to her usually calm and collected character. "It was interesting, the way I chose to play that one," the actress recalls. "Weir's reason for going [to the planet] wasn't out of concern for Sheppard, otherwise she would have gone every other time. There had to be something separate, or it wouldn't make sense. So for me, it had to do with the excitement of the fact that there was Ancient writing and technology there, which is all she cares about. While everyone else is concerned with Sheppard, Weir was just like a kid, excited." She laughs, mimicking the delivery of her lines in the episode, "'and this reads this and this is this and...' Everyone else is saying, 'We've got a time issue here, we've got to save Sheppard...' and she's like, 'Yeah, but this reads this...' It was the first time, for me, where I could show that this is what she cares about. This is what she wanted to do, this is why she's still here, hoping they can get to do more of this. I chose to do it that way, to go, 'She's not going to be serious this time. She's out of the office and she's reading Ancient script, and that's *cool*!'"

"I did the teleplay, and it's not my best work," says Brad Wright candidly of 'Epiphany'. "But I think it is ultimately a good little episode, especially the beginning sections where Sheppard's stuck. I could have written a whole episode about that, and I almost should have. I seem to like just real-time drama, just heaping on the problems and having characters struggle with those kinds of things." Å

CRITICAL MASS

STORY BY: Brad Wright and Carl Binder TELEPLAY BY: Carl Binder DIRECTED BY: Andy Mikita	GUEST CAST: Beau Bridges (Major General Hank Landry), Jaime Ray Newman (Lieutenant Laura Cadman), Ellie Harvie (Dr Lindsey Novak), Ben Cotton (Kavanagh), David Nykl (Dr Radek Zelenka), Bill Dow (Dr Bill Lee), Peter Flemming (Agent Malcolm Barrett), Mitch Pileggi (Colonel Steven Caldwell), Gary Jones (Sergeant Walter Harriman)

Atlantis' long-range sensors pick up two Wraith hives fighting each other, while Teyla discovers that Charin is dying on the mainland and doesn't want treatment. Having had a good life, Charin wants to die peacefully of natural causes. Meanwhile, SGC discovers that the Trust have planted a bomb in Atlantis, set to explode the next time the team dials Earth. SGC manage to let Atlantis know, but then learn that the detonator is in Atlantis too. The problem becomes even more pressing when the city's gate starts dialing Earth on its own and transmitting a distress beacon, which is picked up by the hive ships. Weir begins questioning personnel, starting with Kavanagh, who previously expressed dissatisfaction with her governance of Atlantis. McKay realizes that instead of using explosives, the saboteur has disabled the ZPM's failsafe, and it will explode if it overloads. Dialing Earth would do that, as would raising the city's shield, which they will be forced to do when the hive ships arrive in orbit. The failsafe override has been protected by a code which is hard to break, and when the city's inertial dampeners begin to overload the power module, there is nothing more they can do — they must find the bomber. Weir, convinced the culprit is Kavanagh, reluctantly authorizes Ronon to use force to get the code. Teyla prepares the Athosian burial ritual for Charin as evacuation begins. Eventually, the Atlantis team realize that the Trust operative is actually Caldwell, who has been taken over by a Goa'uld. Fighting the parasite, the Colonel manages to give them the code, which saves the city, leaving Hermiod to try and extract the Goa'uld symbiote.

DR LEE: It's like the twilight bark. *101 Dalmatians*? Didn't you guys see that movie? My kids love it. Well there's all these dogs, and one barks here, one barks here... they send a message across the countryside... *Lord of the Rings*! You know when they light all those signal fires on the mountaintops? You saw that, right?

Opposite: Is there more to Caldwell than meets the eye?

Since the beginning of season one, the Atlantis team had spent so much time

worrying about the Pegasus Galaxy's 'big bad', the Wraith, that they hadn't had much time to think of the older evils they had left behind in Earth's own galaxy. 'Critical Mass' changed all that, whilst also giving several characters a chance to flex their muscles — though not necessarily quite how they expected.

"The whole time as I was reading the script, I was trying to figure out who it was going to be," says Mitch Pileggi with a laugh, "and it was me! The first thing that popped into my mind was, 'Does this mean that I'm going to die?' I thought it was an interesting direction to take it. It was good for the character. It showed a weakness, a horror in moments of not being in control of himself and everything around him, which is big to Caldwell.

"It was a lot of fun playing a Goa'uld and knowing that some of the other characters on these two shows have gone through being taken over by alien entities," the actor continues with another laugh. "The toughest part of the whole episode was just saying 'Goa'uld'! I went to Brad and said, 'How do you say the word?' He said 'Well, just say Elliot Gould,' and I said, 'That's not how everyone else says it! They say "gold" or "gooold" or "ga-u-ld"!'"

McKAY: A deletion point, yes — believe it or not I have had some experience with these systems. More, say, than a tap dancing explosives expert!
CADMAN: I was just trying to help, Rodney.

"'Critical Mass' was far and away the most difficult episode I had to do all season long," reveals Carl Binder, who took charge of writing the script. "It benefited greatly from us having our hiatus in the middle. We started prepping and then we had our hiatus, and then we finished it, which gave us time to do the song, because Rachel had to go down to Los Angeles to record and have it ready for playback for the scenes. Story-wise, it was a hard script to write. It was Brad's initial idea and then I filled it out and did all the rewrites. It was my first episode in charge of seeing it through. It went through a lot of changes and was very complicated. Ultimately, 'Critical Mass' and 'Michael' were my two most satisfying episodes of the season, as far as coming out the way I wanted. I was very pleased, but going through it was really difficult."

It wasn't only hard for the writer. The content of the episode proved controversial for some of the cast, most notably Torri Higginson, who had to reconcile herself to the decisions that Elizabeth Weir would make in trying to secure the safety of Atlantis. "It was very hard for me to play," admits the actress, "because to be honest, as an actor the response was, 'This isn't my character, she would not do this.' And it's so close to being personal, the fact that she does pick Kavanagh, the person that she had an issue with [previously]. It's very difficult. I chose to play it that she does have

support from everyone else on her team, and they are pushing her. There are two or three times where they're saying, 'You've got to do this.' She makes a bad decision, and obviously, as an actor, you want a ripple — to have a scene in the next episode where she's reeling from that. But they've got a lot of characters to explore every week. I think she had one line where she says, 'I crossed a line,' and that was it. What I tried to do was just play the beats in between, what isn't said. To have the look in her eye, the uncomfortable sense of self."

Weir wasn't the only character to struggle with the events of 'Critical Mass'. For Beckett, he discovered that some of the customs of the Athosians on Atlantis were easier to observe than others, particularly when it comes to the Hippocratic oath. "That's an episode where he does have to give in to certain customs that he wouldn't normally do," agrees Paul McGillion. "He really wants to live by the oath he took as a doctor, but in these cases he has to succumb to different races and what their cultures and traditions are. That's interesting, and another dilemma for him. With 'Critical Mass', he's going against every thing that he learnt, but in this sort of situation he has to sit back and observe. I think in some ways that matured him, and opened his eyes to what we're doing here."

One of the most striking aspects of 'Critical Mass' were the lyrics that Carl Binder wrote for Rachel Luttrell to sing at Charin's funeral, which Joel Goldsmith in turn incorporated into the episode's score. Luttrell, a trained singer, had been eager to display her considerable vocal talent in some way on the show, and the executive producer picked this as the perfect opportunity to do so.

"Rachel has such a great voice, and she sang it with that beautiful voice. And I said, 'It's lovely, but it isn't Teyla. Does Teyla sing that well? No! You have to go and do it again!'" Wright laughs. "It's still quite beautiful — it's just more Teyla. The song services the story quite well toward the climax. Carl did a great job. It's a 'pot-boiler' story, things just get hotter and hotter." Å

GRACE UNDER PRESSURE

WRITTEN BY: Martin Gero
DIRECTED BY: Martin Wood

GUEST CAST: Amanda Tapping (Lieutenant Colonel Samantha Carter), David Nykl (Dr Radek Zelenka), William MacDonald (Captain Griffin), Peter Abrams (Lieutenant Donaldson), Nimet Kanji (Dr Bryce)

McKay and Lieutenant Donaldson are returning to Atlantis in a repaired puddle-jumper when the craft pitches into the water. Coming around, the two find themselves in mortal danger as the pressure of the water threatens to crush the small ship as they sink deeper and deeper. The ship's windshield cracks, and Donaldson sacrifices himself to shut McKay in the protected rear compartment. Trying not to panic, McKay struggles to find a way to save himself whilst suffering from a head injury and hypothermia, not to mention rapidly running out of oxygen and power. In the city, Zelenka tries to locate the sunken ship while Sheppard attempts to come up with a rescue plan. The main problem is that the ship could be anywhere after being tugged by the ocean's currents, and is so deep that another jumper cannot reach it without being crushed itself. As McKay's situation worsens and his panic increases, he begins to hallucinate — in particular Lieutenant Colonel Sam Carter, his old sparring partner from SGC and a woman that exercises his imagination whether or not he is suffering from a head injury. 'Carter' tries to persuade him to stop attempting his own rescue — a pretty impossible proposition considering how deep he is under water. She wants him to wait for Sheppard, who has had the idea of turning the rescue jumper's cloak into a shield. McKay's mania becomes more distinct as his injuries worsen, but Carter tries to convince him to trust his teammates. McKay finally relents, which is just as well — if he had implemented his plan he would have died. Instead, Sheppard arrives and projects his jumper's shield around Rodney's, allowing the doctor to leave his hallucination behind and walk to safety.

CARTER: This isn't good.
McKAY: Look, just, just — shut up! You come in here, you don't help me, you say the one plan I've got is bad. You claim to be a creation of my mind, and yet you are in no way dressed provocatively..."

'Grace Under Pressure' was the perfect opportunity to create a 'crossover' between *Stargate: Atlantis* and parent show *Stargate SG-1*. It also provided a way to reunite two characters that hadn't crossed paths for some years, as 'Samantha Carter' took a trip to the bottom of the ocean to help out a stranded Rodney McKay.

Opposite: McKay's fondest wish finally comes true — in his dreams!

"That was *so* much fun," exclaims *Stargate SG-1*'s Amanda Tapping, who spent two days filming under water with David Hewlett at the University of British Columbia for the episode. "I love David Hewlett and I love the dynamic between Carter and McKay. What I love about this script is that it was taken that step further. The snarkiness is fun to play, but there was also a sexual tension underlying it all. Their competition is sibling rivalry with a twist. Carter obviously thinks she's smarter, but they are as quick as each other so they keep each other on their toes, because they have the same interests and they're in the same field."

Written by Martin Gero, the episode was an echo of Damian Kindler's episode 'Grace' for *Stargate SG-1*'s seventh year, in which Carter found herself in a similar predicament aboard the abandoned *Prometheus*.

"Since the end of last year I've been wanting to do something with the water," the writer explains. "The city is surrounded by water, and it looks so great. Over the Christmas break, when I knew I would be working on *Stargate SG-1*, I went and watched seasons five, six and seven. So I saw 'Descent', and I was like, 'This is awesome, why haven't we done this in *Stargate: Atlantis*?' So I came in and said 'I'd love to do a puddle-jumper-sinking-under-water episode.' I had of course seen 'Grace' as well, and Brad said, 'Well, we kind of did the same thing with Sam, but she was able to hallucinate all these characters to help her get out of the situation.' I immediately said, 'Well, if McKay was going to hallucinate anyone, it would be Sam.' And Brad was like, 'Grace Under Pressure!'" The writer laughs, "I never thought we'd call it that for real!"

McKAY: You are very clever. I would even give you brilliant. But there's brilliant, and then there's *me*.
CARTER: Every time we've worked together, you've been wrong and I've been right.

Having come up with what seemed to be the perfect way to reunite the two old sparring partners, Gero enthusiastically got to work on the script. Though he had written his first episode of *Stargate SG-1* by completing 'The Ties That Bind' for season nine, Gero had never written for Carter herself. "I'm a big Carter fan," says the writer. "The McKay episodes with her are spectacular. So for 'Grace Under Pressure', I watched those three episodes again, because I was less worried about nailing Sam's voice than I was getting Sam's voice *with* McKay. I felt I had a little bit of leeway because [here] she is a figment of his imagination. I felt a freedom there, and that kind of Spencer Tracey/Audrey Hepburn back-and-forth is so much fun to write. I was really nervous to see what Amanda would think about it, or even if she would do it, because it was up in the air whether she was going to have the time. She did it essentially as a favor and to have fun with it."

Of course, as has become customary, David Hewlett found himself at the sharp end of Martin Gero's writing, charged with delivering page after page of dialogue direct to camera. The writer has nothing but praise for how well the actor pulled off the script, though writing it proved just as taxing as delivering the lines. "It was just a really difficult episode to write because for two acts you have McKay in the back of a jumper alone," Gero explains. "It was easy to write scenes for just David Hewlett when he was in 'Duet' on his own because he had two characters inside him so he could play two parts. But I always think it's cheesy when people talk out loud to themselves! So I would be down on the set for whatever reason and people would ask, 'What are you writing at the moment?' and I'd say, 'Ugh! I'm stuck in the back of a jumper with McKay. I have to write another ten pages of him talking by himself!' But, not to be overly complementary to David Hewlett, because he already has a massive out-of-control ego," Gero jokes, "he did essentially a ten-page monologue in the back of that jumper in one day. We shot all that stuff, those two acts alone with him in *one day*!"

"I talk so fast!" laughs David Hewlett. "Normally our days are six or seven pages. And then it's a 'McKay Dialogue Day' and we shoot ten! Everyone says, 'Oh my god, how do you do it?' It's actually easier, because there's no one else to screw up the lines. You know exactly what you are supposed to say next. I love it, although I still think the strength of the show is the banter between people. I think it was a very clever device to have Amanda personified so that it isn't just McKay talking to himself all the time. If you've got a couple of guys talking in a puddle-jumper, it can feel a little stretched after twenty minutes. But it's got the back and forth between Atlantis and the jumper and the banter between Amanda and me — it's a very cleverly crafted script. And then [director] Martin Wood has this great way of turning scenes that you think will be [simple] into all these great cuts back and forth and strange off-angles. So it's actually much more dynamic than I expected it to be. There's a lot more motion in it."

"The junior editor is the unsung hero in this episode," adds Gero. "There was hours of useable footage. We could have made three very different episodes from all the stuff we had. But I think we got the best one." Å

THE TOWER

WRITTEN BY: Joseph Mallozzi & Paul Mullie

DIRECTED BY: Andy Mikita

GUEST CAST: Mark Gibbon (Constable), Richard Kahan (Baldric), Anna Cummer (Petra), Jay Brazeau (Lord Protector), Chelan Simmons (Mara), Brendan Beiser (Tavius), David Bloom (Eldred), Peter Woodward (Otho)

Sheppard's team visits a society 'protected' by something called "The Tower". When the team investigate, they discover a structure rising from the earth of the planet that looks suspiciously similar to the central spire of their own city. The protection offered by the spire is actually many controlled drones — which, if the Lord Protector is willing to trade with Atlantis, would mean they could replenish Atlantis' supplies. However, the inhabitants of the Tower are selfish and greedy, constantly demanding tithes that keep their people in poverty. Sheppard attracts the attention of Otho, Chamberlain to the Lord Protector. He is taken to the Tower, and discovers a sick ruler holding court with a decadent group of privileged wastrels. It is clear that the Lord Protector and his bloodline have the ancient gene, but it is waning with each generation. The Chamberlain has discovered Sheppard's own genetic structure, and plans to marry him to the Lord Protector's willing daughter, Mara, much to the chagrin of her brother, Tavius, who wants the throne for himself in exchange for some drones. Sheppard tries to persuade the Chamberlain that what they actually need instead is a better system of government, and tells him about the gene therapy Atlantis can provide. Meanwhile, McKay has found a way into the Ancient city, from where he can shut down the ZPM that gives the ruling class its power. When the Lord Protector dies, the Chamberlain's true nature emerges — far from being a liberal servant, he plans to marry Mara himself and become Lord Chamberlain, and arrests both Tavius and Sheppard for treason. McKay realizes that the city is almost out of ZPM power, but can't disconnect it because a cave-in has trapped him in another part of the buried city. Instead he activates the stardrive, draining the power while, during a struggle with Sheppard, Otho is accidentally killed — with his own poison.

MARA: What you said at dinner — did you mean it?
SHEPPARD: Absolutely. What did I say again?

With the added security of knowing that season one had performed so well, the writers and producers felt able to experiment a little more for season two, trying different approaches to keep the series form invigorated. One such episode was 'The Tower', a distinct departure from the style and format of previous episodes. It was the brainchild of writing team Paul Mullie and Joseph Mallozzi, though it was Mullie who took the lead in writing the script. "The story evolved from something Joe

Opposite: Why are the bad guys always British?

originally pitched," the writer explains, "the idea of finding a 'sister city' to Atlantis. That is, we step through the gate into an identical gateroom, meet the people who live there, think they might be Ancients, then realize that in fact they're distant descendants, who through inbreeding have a) lost the ability to control the city's systems and b) become corrupt and evil, with a penchant for cruelly lording it over the peasants who don't have the same bloodline. Somewhere along the way, we decided that it would be better if we started outside the city, meet the peasants first, then reveal the city at the end of the tease. Then that evolved into the idea that the city was mostly buried, and that the big reveal in the tease would be a *Planet of the Apes*, Statue of Liberty-like image of just the top portion of the central tower sticking up from the forest. And so we had our title."

'The Tower' was directed by Andy Mikita, who enjoyed the challenge involved in presenting such a different story to the audience. He admits, however, that creating the episode also carried with it a whole set of worries for the production: "'The Tower' was a lot of fun, very different. There was a calculated risk involved in terms of the concept and premise behind it. There was a lot that I was unsure about at the beginning. From the script, I was like, 'Well, this is cool...' but with a little bit of hesitation because I wasn't sure if I got it. So there's always a little bit of apprehension there. But I think it turned out to be fun."

McKAY: I'm not interested in your primitive taboos, okay? It's a dark and scary place, but it's not cursed or haunted or anything like that. It's perfectly safe.
BALDRIC: Actually, the catacombs are prone to earthquakes.

"It is quite different from the usual style of *Stargate*, and as a result, I think it put some people off," Mullie acknowledges. "We kind of knew that might happen going in, but what the hell, you can't do the same stuff week in and week out. Even people who like the more formulaic 'inside the box' episodes would eventually get bored with them. What I've always liked about *Stargate* is the fact that we're not afraid to mix it up, that you never know week to week what kind of episode you're going to get. What happened with this one was that we were really behind the eight-ball in terms of prep time, particularly with respect to wardrobe. We wound up having to rent most of it, which is why it looks pretty different from the stuff we usually do. It was quite over-the-top, so we decided that instead of fighting it, we would embrace it, and make this an over-the-top episode in general, reveling in the wackiness of it. Hence the banquet scene, the seduction scene, the general technicolor quality of the whole episode. Look at the flamboyant performance of the guy who played Tavius (Brendan Beiser). In an

Above: The villagers have
good reason to watch the
skies.

outfit like that, how else are you going to play it? I thought he was hilarious."

Another guest star that particularly impressed both the writer and director was the actor who played Otho, the devious chamberlain eager to take a position of power. "What really grounded it was the performance of Peter Woodward," say Mullie. "He lent the whole thing a seriousness that kept it from getting completely out of hand. That was a much more subtle character. He had to be scary at first, then sympathetic, then kind of creepy, and finally full-on evil, and I think he pulled it off amazingly well." Å

MISSION Å DEBRIEF

SGC

Ancient Super-Weapon

The 'throne' that the Lord Protector uses to wield such absolute power and terror over his subjects is actually the control seat of a weapon of great magnitude, first discovered by SG-1 on Earth in the outpost at Antarctica that eventually led Dr Daniel Jackson to find a way to the city of Atlantis. Operated by those possessing the Ancient gene, the super-weapon (at its peak) is equipped with thousands of independent nodules known as 'drones', each of which packs a powerful explosive power of its own. The operator, seated in the chair, can control these drones with his or her mind. The power of the weapon was demonstrated during the showdown that SG-1 participated in between Anubis' approaching ship and Earth's own fledgling spaceship. Without the super-weapon, Earth's forces could not have defended against the attack, but with it they were able to level the field and destroy the system lord's fleet. Atlantis is also equipped with such a super-weapon, though its stock of drones is depleted. The team is thus always on the lookout for a way to replenish their supply.

THE LONG GOODBYE

WRITTEN BY: Damian Kindler
DIRECTED BY: Andy Mikita

GUEST CAST: Kavan Smith (Major Lorne),
Mitch Pileggi (Colonel Steven Caldwell)

Sheppard's team detects two life signs — one male, one female — in small pods orbiting a planet. Transporting them to Atlantis, the decision is taken to open one of the pods. It reveals an old woman, close to death. Weir steps closer, wondering who she is, and is grabbed by some kind of beam emanating from the pod. When she comes round, Weir appears to be no longer in control of her own body. The consciousness of the old woman, who calls herself Phoebus, tells them she is willing to relax control so that Weir can address her team. 'Elizabeth' tells them that the other pod holds the body of Phoebus' husband, Thalen. Opening the other pod will activate the beam and transfer her husband's consciousness into whoever is close enough for just long enough for them to bid each other a last goodbye. 'Weir' asks Sheppard to do the honors. He agrees rather reluctantly — but when the transfer takes place, it quickly becomes apparent that Phoebus was lying. She and Thalen are actually sworn enemies who want one last chance to wipe each other out. Breaking out of the room, they go on the rampage, using Weir and Sheppard's knowledge of the base to escape capture. As Phoebus' violent determination to kill Thalen escalates, she attempts to use the lives of the Atlantis personnel as collateral, before trying to force Teyla to pull the trigger on Sheppard's controlled body. Caldwell and the other Atlantis personnel attempt to regain control of the base, and McKay eventually manages to lock out Weir's passwords. Thalen's hold on Sheppard disintegrates, though Teyla refuses to believe him. However, when Phoebus arrives, intent on killing Teyla's 'unconscious' captive, Sheppard stuns her. Next morning, Sheppard and Weir have returned to normal — though Weir's embarrassment will take longer to fade.

McKAY: You two need some very serious marriage counseling.

PHOEBUS: He's not my husband, he's the enemy. Now drop your weapon.

One of the most memorable episodes of the season, 'The Long Goodbye' was another very different *Stargate: Atlantis* episode. For a start, writer/producer Damian Kindler had originally pitched it as a *Stargate SG-1* story.

"It was funny because the story was born literally the week before my second daughter came into this world in June '05," he recalls. "I was chatting with Rob

Opposite: Nice women can be tough too!

THE LONG GOODBYE

[Cooper] about how ancient cultures used to send their two best warriors to decide an important battle. I thought it would be cool to find two people in stasis and unfreeze them — only to discover they want to kill each other. Rob casually mentioned it would probably make a better *Stargate: Atlantis* than *Stargate SG-1* (he does that). I shrugged and then went out to eat Mexican food with Andy Mikita. I came back to the production office an hour later and saw Brad in the hallway. He said that Rob had mentioned my two warriors idea and he wanted to do it. Things kind of went from there."

Director Andy Mikita was charged with putting the episode together, and relished giving actress Torri Higginson a chance to finally show Weir holding a weapon. "She had a ball with that," says Mikita with a laugh. "She really created that altered character, really went to town with it. She had the little piece of hair dangling in front of her eyes, the attitude — Torri brought in a different character that was really cool, and I know that she worked very hard on that. It was a tough episode for her, not just because of the obvious components — the second character, the fact that she was firing a gun and she'd never done that before — but also the way in which we shot that episode. It was just spread out all over the place. It was almost a running joke: "The Long Goodbye', the episode that will never end!' We never seemed to be able to get all our days finished. We would shoot a sequence and have a regular scheduled day, but we wouldn't quite finish up. It was a great big ambitious script and we didn't have any additional time to shoot it, so we were certainly aware that we were going to run into some problems. Just the way things got scheduled, if we didn't finish a day then the scene that we had dropped would have to be done three weeks down the road, and that happened continuously through the course of that episode. It was very frustrating, particularly for Torri because there were days where they would be on a completely different episode, [for example] doing 'Aurora' for two thirds of the day and then all of a sudden the last scene of the day is going to be from 'The Long Goodbye' and it might be a really emotional scene. So it was hard to twist back into that mind set. But I thought she did an extraordinary job. I loved the character that she created, and she did a great job with the gunfire."

THALEN: If you kill me, you're killing him. He cares for you more than you know.

TEYLA: Please do not make me do this.

"I just had so much fun doing 'The Long Goodbye'," enthuses Higginson. "I used to do a lot of action stuff years ago and I haven't done it for years. It was just really fun to be able to play something very different. The writers are wonderful in how they do that. Each actor gets a 'bone' thrown at them every year — one episode that just allows them to have a lot of fun. And that was mine for that year! And it was a great challenge, too, because we shot it about two episodes before it was scheduled to shoot. BamBam

Above: Sheppard fights for his life against an unlikely foe.

(stunt coordinator James Bamford) and I had spoken about him teaching me this fight routine, and he said, 'It's based on the one from *The Bourne Supremacy*.' so I was watching that going, 'There's no *way* I'm going to be able to do that! But at least we'll have a month to rehearse it.' And then the next thing they're saying, 'Okay, you're shooting in three days!' But I like that, too. I like the 'guerilla film-making' that happens with doing a television series sometimes. You don't have the rehearsal and you just have to dive in and give 110 per cent," she laughs, "and hope that they can fix it in editing!"

"One of my favorite days of shooting was on that episode," recalls actor David Hewlett, "because you've got 'Mum and Dad' abducted by alien consciousnesses and trying to shoot each other in the basement of Atlantis, and there's Caldwell and Beckett and McKay, and what do they do? Well, they just start screaming at each other," he laughs. "We had this day, literally, where we were just killing ourselves [laughing], because every scene just erupted in complete panic. We didn't know what to do, everyone has a different idea of what we should do, and everyone starts arguing about who should be in command. It's a great descent into chaos as soon as the two leaders are taken out of the picture. And they've got this great *Mr. & Mrs. Smith* thing happening. That's going to be a classic episode, for sure. It was a fantastic script."

Mitch Pileggi also enjoyed filming the episode for the same reason — the total insanity which overtakes the control room as the rest of the Atlantis team try to work out how to stop Weir and Sheppard murdering each other. "I had quite a lot of stuff with McKay and we had so much fun," he says. "As soon as Weir and Sheppard are taken out of the picture, everything goes haywire. We're screaming at each other, and no one knows what anyone else is doing. And trying to control it is mass chaos. We were laughing so hard — we had a lot of fun with that."

For Brad Wright, however, the humor of the episode was balanced nicely by the darker aspects of the story. "There are elements of humor in it, but it's on the edge," he points out. "They're not horrible people, they just want to win. It's a 100 year-old battle they've been waging and they want there to be a winner. But again, there's that little touch of darkness — people get hurt pretty badly." Å

COUP D'ETAT

WRITTEN BY: Martin Gero
DIRECTED BY: Martin Wood

GUEST CAST: Ryan Robbins (Ladon Radim), Colm Meaney (Cowen), Penelope Corrin (Dr Lindsay), Sonja Bennett (Dahlia Radim), Kavan Smith (Major Lorne)

L orne's team is attacked while off world, and when Sheppard's team investigates, they find what seem to be the burnt corpses of the Atlantis personnel. The resulting briefing back in Atlantis is interrupted by a communication from Ladon of the Genii, one of Kolya's strike force who tried to take the city by force the previous year. They have monitored the movements of teams returning to Atlantis and know that the city is still intact. Weir faces Ladon, who claims to have a ZPM. Ladon refuses to talk to anyone but Weir, and when he does so, asks for weaponry in return for the ZPM. The Genii have become a nuclear power under Cowen, who Ladon wants to depose before he can do anything rash. Weir, after considering, decides to strengthen Atlantis' position with Cowen instead of helping Ladon, and sends McKay and Sheppard to see the Genii and warn him of the impending coup. Sheppard, having sent men to follow Ladon, plans to steal the ZPM by inviting some of Ladon's group to Atlantis for supplies while his team attack their hideout. Weir agrees, and when Ladon's people arrive through the gate they are taken prisoner. On Ladon's planet, however, Sheppard realizes they have been duped — Ladon is waiting for them and the ZPM is dead. The prisoners in Atlantis are all willing sacrifices, terminally ill from radiation sickness. Ladon is really working with Cowen, who contacts Weir and demands Atlantis' jumpers in return for her personnel's lives — including McKay, Sheppard and Lorne, who was captured to provide a sample of the Ancient gene. Weir reports to Cowen and Ladon that Beckett can cure the prisoners they are holding. Cowen doesn't care, but Ladon's sister is among the group — and he reveals that he really is planning a coup against Cowen, and detonates a nuclear weapon that wipes out the leader. Ladon lets the team go and Beckett cures his countrymen. Weir, offering the rest of the Genii medical treatment, is happy that they may finally have reached a friendly accord.

McKAY: Are we in some sort of trouble?
SHEPPARD: Was it the gas or the prison cell that was your first clue?

"I felt like I spent half of the year writing 'Coup D'Etat'," says Martin Gero with a laugh. "I finished 'Grace Under Pressure' before our summer hiatus in June, and so I started 'Coup D'Etat' before the hiatus. We wanted to do another Genii episode this year, and after [writing] 'The Brotherhood' and 'The Storm' and 'The Eye', I kind of

Opposite: Teyla discovers that some of her friends are on a worrying list.

felt a little bit of ownership over them, so I wanted to do another episode.

"It was originally going to bring back Robert Davi (Kolya) and Colm Meaney (Cowen), and have Robert Davi take over as the leader of the Genii. So I wrote it, and it was difficult. And then we found out that not only was Robert Davi not available, but Colm Meaney was not available! So it was kind of an 'Oh, shit' moment.

"I went back and re-wrote it with Ladon, who was a Genii in 'The Storm' and 'The Eye'… and it was terrible! It was bad because when you're using two existing characters, you don't really spend a lot of time in exposition to figure out who these people are. The amount of people you had to add to that script to make sense — to not only introduce two new characters, but explain where the two characters we know went — was substantial. So Brad read it and was like, 'Well, this is bad.' And I was like, 'I know!'

"Thankfully, 'The Long Goodbye' was in pretty good shape at that point — and 'Coup D'Etat' had already been pushed [back]. We pushed it because of set requirements for 'Michael', and then when Brad read it and realized that it was no good without Colm Meaney and Robert Davi, he said, 'Well, when is either of them available?' So we called both of their managers and discovered that Colm had an availability at the very end of the schedule if we slotted it in the [episode] 218 slot. So then we pulled 'The Long Goodbye' up again and pushed 'Coup D'Etat' down. So I rewrote it *again*, putting Meaney back into it! So I did more drafts of that script than I have ever done for *Stargate: Atlantis* before. So at the end of it, I was like 'God, I'm so sick of this episode. This episode is so boring and dumb.' But I saw a cut of it and actually it's a pretty good episode!"

DEX: Sheppard's on the list, McKay is on the list. Why aren't Teyla and me?
WEIR: What, you're feeling left out?
DEX: I just want to know who thinks I'm not a threat and give them a chance to change their mind.

In the end, thanks to the eventual availability of Colm Meaney, executive producer Brad Wright agrees. "I don't mind enemies being smart and getting one up on us," says Wright. "We get out of our situations by being who we are — it's either some element of our humanity, or we're appealing to some aspect of their humanity. If it's the Genii, that's what saves us, not our deviousness or counter deviousness, as it were. It's a great story."

Torri Higginson also enjoyed 'Coup D'Etat' as a way to illustrate just why Weir is such a valuable asset to the Atlantis mission. For every episode where Weir's platitudes save a situation, there are episodes like this to show that the doctor can be just as tough as her military colleagues when she needs to be.

Above: Sheppard, a friend of the Genii?

"What I like, especially about 'Coup D'Etat', was that there was negotiation going on. There was a play of politics happening. I enjoy it when they write that stuff for Weir, because I think that's where you see her strengths shine through. At times, people can question, 'Why has this woman been put in this position?' She's not military, she doesn't have the experience, and so when they give me those sorts of negotiation scenes and those political moments — those are the moments where you understand why Weir's there, when you're dealing with language or culture or you're dealing with diplomacy. Even though the diplomacy is getting less diplomatic. The Genii are human, but everything has shifted because of their struggles and their distrust. Everyone is in this fight-or-flight scenario, trying to survive as best they can." The actress laughs suddenly, and adds, "I was sad though, because I didn't actually get to act with Colm Meaney! All of our stuff was over the video. I was like, 'Oh! But I want to act with him!'" Å

MISSION DEBRIEF
SGC

The Genii

The Genii have frequently shown themselves to be masters of deception. Teyla Emmagan first introduced the Atlantis team to the Genii, believing them to be simple farmers who would provide good trade partners for the city. She herself had been trading with them on behalf of her own people for a good many years, and had no suspicions that they were anything other than the agrarian culture they purported to be. As Sheppard and McKay discovered, however, this quiet life hid a society with dark ambitions of developing their own nuclear device with which to destroy the Wraith. When this plan failed and Sheppard's team managed to escape, the Genii instigated a feud with Atlantis. Planning to take it over while it ran on a skeleton crew, General Kolya invaded the city with a group of his men (including Ladon), and following the defeat of that plan, stalked Sheppard's team in order to steal a ZPM Atlantis desperately needed. Since then, until Ladon's takeover, the Genii had been out of contact with Atlantis, dealing with their losses at the hands of a Wraith culling. Though they now seem to have reached a state of alliance with Atlantis, it remains to be seen whether their deceptions are at an end.

MICHAEL

WRITTEN BY: Carl Binder
DIRECTED BY: Martin Wood

GUEST CAST: Connor Trinneer (Michael Kenmore),
Claire Rankin (Dr Kate Heightmeyer)

A young man wakes up in the Atlantis infirmary, connected to many wires and monitors. Weir calls him Lieutenant Michael Kenmore, but he himself has no memory. The Atlantis crew tell him that he was a member of one of their teams captured by the Wraith, but they aren't sure what it is that they have done to him. He is told that he has been unconscious for days. As his stay in the infirmary continues, Beckett keeps in contact with the rest of the team, informing them of his progress. Michael is having a hard time adjusting now that he is awake and out in the larger community, but latches on to Teyla, seeming to remember her as a friend. Others, however, find dealing with him difficult — particularly Ronon. Eventually, Michael realizes through his disturbed dreams that something is not right. Determined to find out the truth, which he feels is being hidden from him, Michael steals some infirmary videotapes — and discovers that he is in fact a Wraith that has been returned to human form by use of Beckett's retrovirus. Outraged, Michael confronts the team, who try to convince him that their decision was right. He tries to escape, killing a guard in the process, but is caught and given the option of continuing the retrovirus treatments or being executed. Michael uses Teyla's compassion for him and guilt at his treatment to take her hostage and escape, taking Teyla with him to a Wraith-inhabited planet. The Atlantis team pursues him, and manages to retrieve Teyla — but Michael, who is now on his way to regaining his full Wraith self, returns to his own kind.

TEYLA: You may not understand this now, but making you human — I believe that this could make your life better.
MICHAEL: Really? From what I was told, you made me human in order to make your lives better. So tell me then, what makes being human better than being a Wraith?

With 'Michael', *Stargate: Atlantis* entered darker territory than it had ever attempted before, and the episode's consequences would be far reaching, both for Atlantis and the characters that had come to call the city home.

"'Michael' is a very dark episode," Brad Wright agrees. "It's not clear cut at all, and in fact it really comes back to bite us in the ass. If there is a theme to this season,

Opposite: Ronon expresses his opinion of Michael's humanity.

Above: Michael (Connor Trinneer) turns the tables on Teyla.

it's that some of our plans, especially our darker ones, come back to snap at us. It begins with us following a person who we believe is a lieutenant, one of our soldiers, and he's just been rescued from the Wraith and he can't remember who he is. The twist, of course, is that he is a Wraith, whom we have given the retrovirus to, and it's caused complete amnesia, which we've just used to our advantage. But he finds out, and he escapes, and that opens the door for the Wraith to come back."

The episode was particularly difficult for actress Torri Higginson, who once again saw Weir being forced to make decisions that went against her nature and conscience. Higginson feels that at the root of Weir's desire to develop the retrovirus remained a basic sense of altruism that has always been the character's main trait. "I had to get my head around it," the actress admits. "I think there's a romantic idealism that both Beckett and her share that, 'Well, actually, could we not be helping them, because they do originally come from humans?' [The Wraith are] an evolution that has happened, but what makes it a positive? Who grades a positive or negative evolution? And as a human you go, 'Well, that's a negative evolution, because you guys now want to kill people.' But from the scientific side, it's just evolution, and there is no judgment, right or wrong. As humans we eat animals — so is that an issue too? There are a lot of gray areas. And I think it's fun to play in the gray area."

"We're tampering with things and I think it's very confusing for him and especially Dr Weir," agrees Paul McGillion, of his own character's reaction to the events of 'Michael'. "She's primarily the political leader and she wants to make sure we're not tampering with different societies when we go to these worlds. It's a tricky plotline to work. I'm happy with it in some regards, but in other regards — you don't want Beckett to come across as Dr Frankenstein. I read 'Michael' initially and thought, 'This is heavy, this is *really* heavy.' He's waking up and he's finding a family that doesn't really exist and everyone's talking to him and saying he has amnesia, but he doesn't. You've got to feel for the character, and a lot of it is a tribute to Connor's portrayal. He did such a fantastic job of bringing out the humanity but being a Wraith at the same time, so that you feel for this guy. It definitely makes for interesting television, that's for sure. It's not light-hearted fare."

TEYLA: It is not too late. We can still go back. Dr Beckett can give you an injection, take away the pain.
MICHAEL: No! This is how it's supposed to be. I'm returning to what I was — what I *am.*

Another character who struggled in the wake of Michael's transformation was Teyla Emmagan, who finds herself having to overcome her natural revulsion for the Wraith in order to convince him of the lie he is being told. As the story progresses, however, it becomes apparent that Teyla is undergoing something of a transformation herself. "'Michael' is actually one of my favorite episodes of the season," reveals Rachel Luttrell, "because of the whole moralistic question. Teyla was in a very odd place because she finds herself having sympathy towards this character. There is a kind of friendship that sparks from that, and I think she did actually develop in that show. She got to see a human side of the Wraith. The enemy is much more interesting if they are not totally evil, if they have different levels and shades.

"I like the whole notion of the fact that Teyla has Wraith DNA herself," the actress continues. "There were some scenes in 'Michael' that were interesting because he sensed something about her, which made her deal with the fact that maybe there is something of them in her." Å

INFERNO

WRITTEN BY: Carl Binder
DIRECTED BY: Peter DeLuise

GUEST CAST: Kevin McNulty (Chancellor Lycus),
Brandy Ledford (Norina), David Nykl (Dr Radek Zelenka),
Mitch Pileggi (Colonel Steven Caldwell)

Sheppard and his team answer a call for assistance from a planet called Taranis. Their Ancient shield generator seems to be failing, and they want help correcting the fault. McKay gets to work while Chancellor Lycos gives Sheppard a tour of the underground facility, which is plagued by seismic tremors. The facility is powered by geothermic energy, and McKay realizes the failure of the shield may be linked to the quakes. Meanwhile, Sheppard discovers that along with all the other technology, the facility also has a non-functioning *Aurora*-class ship. Weir hopes that by opening negotiations, Atlantis might eventually be allowed access to the ship. McKay is shocked to discover that the shield has been running off geothermic energy continuously for a year, which has overloaded the failsafe. The facility is built above a super-volcano which has been awakened by the shield activity. He recommends evacuation, but Lycos refuses, believing that it is a ruse by Atlantis to take control of the Ancient ship. Eventually he has no choice, but as the people begin to leave, the Stargate is lost in a sea of lava. The whole team, apart from Weir, Lycos and the first group of evacuees, is trapped on the planet. Weir orders the *Daedalus* to divert to Taranis, but it's not big enough to hold everyone. Back on the planet Sheppard orders McKay to try and fix the Ancient ship, which they re-name the *Orion*. McKay tries to get it to fly as Teyla and Ronon round up the last of the population. Some of them are unwilling to leave, thinking they can outrun the volcano, and by waiting, Teyla and Ronon cut themselves off from the *Orion*, but the *Daedalus* arrives in time to beam them from the surface. Sheppard, looking for Teyla and Ronon, finds himself trapped as the facility locks down. Rodney, failing to get the engines working, decides to rely on the shields, which should hold for just long enough for him to open a hyperspace window and jump the ship into orbit. It works — just, but Taranis is lost in a dust cloud.

McKAY: I have a very firm grasp of Ancient technology!
SHEPPARD: You've blown up entire *planets*, Rodney.

Opposite: Sheppard and Norina (Brandy Ledford) realize they may have a problem.

Traditionally, the penultimate episode of a television series, particularly an action-adventure one like *Stargate: Atlantis*, is designed to save money. This is usually so the season finale can be a huge, blowout affair. With 'Inferno', the production once again broke the mold and decided to create a story involving one of the most difficult elements to emulate on screen — a volcano.

"I thought that it would be difficult to get the lava thing going," recalls director Peter DeLuise of his first impressions of the script. "It is difficult, and it is expensive. The movement of lava is very difficult to achieve in CG; it's like a liquid, but a little bit more solid, and also like fur."

WEIR: You asked for our help, and we came.
LYCOS: To fix out shield generator, not incite the evacuation of our planet.

"The element of it that I was really hooked on at the beginning ended up being taken out of the episode, which I thought was pretty funny," says Carl Binder, with a laugh. "Robert [Cooper] had mentioned that he wanted to do an episode about the *Daedalus* being used as a lifeboat. We go to a planet in distress and about to be destroyed by natural causes, and there's only enough room on the *Daedalus* for so many people. So which people get to go and which people have to stay behind and die? I said, 'That sounds really good, I want to do that one.' So I started working, and at some point along the way — and a lot of this had to do with budgetary reasons — that element ended up being removed. The episode became a race against time."

The episode wasn't an easy one to get right on paper, let alone on screen, as Binder explains. "The first outline that I turned in, everybody freaked out because it was so huge," chuckles the writer. "I had Caldwell actually landing the *Daedalus*, people rushing onto the ship and then an eruption. And as the *Daedalus* is starting to sink into the lava, they fire the engines and shoot out. It was just a big, colossal episode. So Brad said, 'Okay, this is really good, but we have to take about ten-million dollars out of it!'

MISSION ⏀ DEBRIEF
SGC

Geothermal Energy

As Earth in the 21st Century struggles to find a way to develop a sustainable, clean energy that will do no further damage to the environment, it seems that the Ancients discovered and implemented a solution more than 10,000 years ago. Geothermal energy makes use of the natural energy expended by a planet's molten core, by channeling the heat given off into power, usually by means of steam or hot water. The Ancients, with their vastly superior technology, knew how to safely transform that energy and run vast complexes, such as the one on Taranis, efficiently for many years. Mindful of the activity they could be causing within the dormant volcano, however, the Ancients established a failsafe that would alert the user to imminent overload. Unfortunately, the Taranians did not understand enough either about geothermal energy or the Ancient language to read the warning signs in enough time to save their home — or the planet.

So I think I did three outlines and two drafts of the script, and by the time I was done with it, Brad walked into my office and said, 'You've taken it *way* too far back. Now it's just a bunch of people standing in a room!' So mercifully, he took it over and did the final rewrite of the script, where he added in various elements and it ended up being a very big episode. That was a strange experience, writing that one!"

As viewers can see from the finished result, 'Inferno' is a big story very well told on the small screen, with effects that rival the biggest-budget movies. This was helped by decisions taken later in the day to reinstate some of the more expensive scenes that had previously been thought too large to attempt within budget. "We cut a bunch of sequences that we thought would be too cost prohibitive," DeLuise explains. "But then Brad Wright, correctly so, decided to add some sequences that had the threat and presence of the lava right there. You *had* to feel the danger of that, and if you didn't the episode wasn't going to work. So he added shots and increased the budget. It made the show worth watching."

"It's one of those ticking-clock, man-versus-nature stories," says executive producer Brad Wright. "It's fun! We also find an *Aurora*-class ship that was in a hangar in the base."

It was less fun for actress Rachel Luttrell, who found herself filming whilst surrounded by air full of gray 'ash', pumped into the set before each take. "That was pretty awful, actually," she says. "All of our crew were walking around with their masks on, and we weren't able to do that. There were moments where Teyla was coughing because she's been breathing ash that is falling out of the sky — and my coughing was real," Luttrell laughs. "Peter DeLuise kept going, 'The coughing is fabulous,' and I was like, 'It's real!' It was difficult to film in."

For Carl Binder, however, the final result was worth all the pain — both in the writers' room and during filming. "It wasn't that the story wasn't working, it was always 'How much can we do so it doesn't look like we're cutting corners?' In the end, we did go over budget. It's a big, very impressive episode. There are some really different kinds of effects that we've never done before — the whole Stargate sinking into the lava is pretty cool!" Å

ALLIES

WRITTEN BY: Martin Gero
DIRECTED BY: Andy Mikita

GUEST CAST: Mitch Pileggi (Colonel Steven Caldwell),
Brent Stait (Michael Kenmore), Andee Frizzell (Wraith Queen),
James Lafazanos (Wraith Scientist)

Anxiously awaiting the arrival of the approaching hive, Atlantis tries to prepare. But instead of attacking, the Wraith send an audio signal asserting that the hive knows Atlantis is there, means them no harm, and they must respond. When they establish a connection, Michael explains that civil war has broken out amongst the Wraith because of lack of food. The solution is for Atlantis to give them the retrovirus, which they will use on their enemies to create a new food source. In exchange, Michael offers the jamming frequency of every hive ship, which when cracked will allow Atlantis the ability to beam a nuclear warhead onto any ship. Alternatively, if Atlantis does not agree with the hive's request, they will tell the rest of the Wraith population that the city is still intact. After a conference, Weir and her team realize that they have no choice but to comply. Beckett will work with the Wraith scientists to 'perfect' the retrovirus. At first the plan goes well, and when the retrovirus is proved to work, the Queen demands a test on a hive within jumping distance of Atlantis. The *Daedalus* attends to monitor their progress. However, the plan backfires when the virus is discovered and the enemy hive fires on Atlantis' 'ally'. The *Daedalus* provides cover for their escape, but as a result Michael's hive demands a better delivery system. McKay is forced to assist, but demands an upload of information about Wraith technology to work from. The Wraith agree, and McKay manages to find a way to get to the hive systems. Another test is necessary, so he volunteers to accompany the hive with Ronon as protection. However, it becomes apparent that the upload from the Wraith ship contains a virus that finds its way into Atlantis' database, giving the Wraith the location of every world in their files. The *Daedalus* is attacked, and Sheppard's F-302 disappears, Ronon and McKay are imprisoned, Atlantis is vulnerable… and Earth, which is all the Wraith ever wanted, is at stake.

WRAITH: Without your help, this damage may have been irreparable.
McKAY: Ah, finally an alien race that appreciates me!

As the time came for *Stargate: Atlantis* to wind up its second season, it rapidly became clear that the finale episode would need to be something particularly special — and very, very dark. With the events of episodes such as 'Critical Mass' and 'Michael', a benchmark had been set for the series that producer Martin Gero found himself charged with living up to for the final story of the year.

Opposite: Sheppard and Caldwell consider their options.

"We had no idea how to end the season," Gero explains. "We knew that potentially it was the Wraith going to Earth, but we didn't know how. So I pitched the idea that [with] a Wraith civil war going on, one of the hives came to us and said, 'Look, we're getting our asses kicked, we need your help.' Brad thought it was maybe too early, that that type of story was more [for] season three. But once we did 'Michael', it just made all the sense in the world. When Michael gets away, you know what's going to happen."

Though the story now fitted perfectly into the framework of the show's second season, writing the actual script was less of an easy ride. "I was terribly nervous about it." Gero recalls. "Because of construction requirements for 'Inferno', we needed to switch the [delivery] order on them. So I essentially wrote 'Coup D'Etat' and 'Allies' back to back — and I only had six days to write 'Allies', which is not long for a season finale! And it was my first season finale, too."

Thankfully Gero did not have to bear the whole burden himself. "It was a group effort," explains the writer. "We sat in that room, banged it out in about a day and a half, and then we went on our September hiatus. We have a week off for Labor Day, and I flew to Prince Edward Island to see my girlfriend. For four hours in the evening I would just pound out the script. I had to do an act a day, essentially, and it came out really easily. You're always gun shy on those, thinking that maybe it's really easy because it's bad! So I was nervous handing it in, because if it was terrible, we didn't have a lot of time to fix it. It was going to have to go into production three days later! But thankfully, everyone really liked it. Brad did a quick polish, and added a couple more funnies. I'm really happy with how the episode turned out. Introducing a foreign element into our environment and how that affects our team members is always good stuff."

WRAITH: I see you have awakened.
McKAY: Really? I was sort of hoping this was just a nightmare.

Though the writer was pleased with the script, the content of the episode was a little more difficult to deal with for actress Torri Higginson. With 'Allies', Weir found the decisions she had made in 'Michael' coming back to haunt her. "I think it's only when Michael comes back with this idea that they decide to use the retrovirus as an offensive weapon," Higginson explains. "In 'Michael', Weir and Beckett thought, 'Wow, what a great thing, instead of killing all these Wraith we can turn them into humans, we can give them what they need, give them planets and we'll all be friends.' A completely ridiculous idea," she laughs, "but I think that was the impulse behind it."

Though Weir did struggle with the judgment she had to make in 'Allies', the actress thinks there was really no other alternative for the doctor than the one she finally chose. "At the end of the day, we don't actually have a choice," the actress says thoughtfully.

Left: McKay finds himself on the way home — but not in the way he'd like.

"They've said if we don't do this they'll tell the Wraith we're here. We can either run or deal with it. So it's kind of a false discussion, because we have been backed into a corner. It's an awful thought, to realize what we're doing."

Paul McGillion agrees. He feels that Dr Beckett, who despite his altruistic intentions, is at the very root of the Atlantis crew's retrovirus quandary, will struggle with the consequences of his discovery for a very long time. "It's very dark for the show, but especially for the character," he says, "because he's the one that develops it. Let's put it this way, I don't think Beckett gets a lot of sleep in the second half of the season, because he's dealing with this."

"We had to knock the Wraith down a notch or two," adds Brad Wright, "but I wanted to remember what the Wraith's primary goal is. The twist at the end of the episode is that Earth is all they ever wanted, because it's full of people. So they lure us into participating in this experiment of disseminating the retrovirus onto another Wraith ship. The first time it doesn't work, so we try again, and they say, 'This time we're going to open up our database and you'll be able to see everything there is to know about a hive ship.' But in that information they bury a worm that goes through our database and finds the location of Earth and the means to get there, with faster engines — which McKay inadvertently helps them build." The executive producer laughs. "Yeah, it's kind of McKay's fault!"

"I think perhaps he's being a little harsh," David Hewlett protests, with a laugh, "I don't want to say that he doesn't know what he's talking about — but he doesn't know what he's talking about! He sits in his ivory tower up there, blah blah blah... But yes. Again, it's another example. He's not infallible, especially when it comes to learning new things. If he's got the opportunity to dive into some Ancient technology that he knows nothing about, then he's right there. He's constantly diving in well over his head. He usually manages to doggy-paddle out of it but generally causes chaos in the process. Yeah, and I suppose inadvertently it is his fault. Although, you know — I blame Weir for letting him do it... and Caldwell. I blame everyone else!" Å

COLONEL JOHN SHEPPARD

"This is Sheppard. I appreciate you can't hear me, but I don't have a volleyball to talk to, so what the hell."

For John Sheppard, his second year in Atlantis would both begin and end with a bang. Having been plucked quite literally from the jaws of death by the *Daedalus*, Sheppard found himself face to face with Colonel Steven Caldwell, who, as a challenger for Sheppard's military leadership in Atlantis, would provide something of a nemesis throughout the season. Besides Caldwell, Sheppard had plenty of other difficulties to contend with, including Ford's disappearance, his own brush with Beckett's retrovirus, and being inhabited by a violent alien visitor.

For actor Joe Flanigan, playing Sheppard for a second year presented him with numerous chances to expand on the character. For a start, through Weir's insistence, Sheppard, hitherto known on Earth as a bad example for the military in terms of discipline, finds himself promoted to Lieutenant Colonel. "I didn't really have to play it too much," Flanigan reveals, "because it was more symbolic than anything. It didn't really change any of the dynamics, with the exception of having Caldwell as an added element that deals with hierarchy and status. I think that he has a little bit more of a team-player feeling — he's less and less of a soloist and more and more a part of the team. I would hope that that comes out."

Regarding Sheppard's abrasive relationship with Caldwell, Flanigan reports that he couldn't be happier. In terms of the introduction of the *Daedalus* herself, however, Flanigan admits that he was initially less happy to find that Atlantis was no longer as isolated as it had been throughout season one. "I was skeptical about that," says the actor frankly, "because I want limited contact with Earth. What will happen if you have too much contact with Earth [is that] you will have too many avenues of salvation. Potentially, you'll get into the situation where anything that's dangerous or difficult, Earth is easy to access, and they can come back with all sorts of reinforcements and leadership. The excitement of the show is that we are essentially marooned here and we have to become a self-sustained unit. So I was kind of skeptical about that, but it still takes three weeks to go back and forth, so it didn't turn out to be a problem.

"But the presence of [the ship] isn't just physically to take you to another place," Flanigan points out. "It's also a reminder of who you work for. That's an important aspect of it being there, because you will constantly see this hierarchical rub that takes place every time Caldwell shows up. So it's not just a really practical thing that's going to get us out of trouble, or get us to a further destination. It's also [a reminder] — don't forget, you work for the boss. So I think that aspect of it is dramatically important."

Besides dealing with pressures from Earthly sources, Sheppard also found himself coming closer to the Wraith than ever with a storyline that found its roots in 'Instinct'. "I thought it was a great idea," Flanigan recalls. "It was precisely what we needed to do. We

COLONEL JOHN SHEPPARD

had [been] fighting against this enemy for so long, and I think it becomes kind of monolithic and possibly homogenous — it's like, boom, the Wraith. That [episode] opened up a really interesting door, created greater complexities, and also allowed us to fight them on different levels. You have to continually explore that, it can't just be, 'Oh, here come the bad guys. Let's shoot the bad guys.' It also shows the close genetic link there is between us and them. It was a critical episode, and I really liked it. I thought everybody did a great job, and it set up things for 'Conversion' really nicely."

'Conversion', in which Sheppard, infected by a bite from the Wraith girl Ellia, begins to mutate, is one of two episodes that Flanigan picks out as being the most significant for the character in year two. The other is the action-packed 'The Long Goodbye', which saw him possessed by an alien entity. "I think 'Conversion' was the most significant one," says the actor. "Sheppard was allowed to have an emotional arc. And I liked shooting 'The Long Goodbye' quite a bit. I would say those are the most significant. I liked the idea behind 'The Long Goodbye'. I thought it was a great idea, and any time you become a different character, it's a lot of fun. Actually, it's funny — I cited those two examples, and those were the only two episodes where I was allowed to become a different character. So that's fun to do. And you don't get to do it that much."

Although 'The Long Goodbye' saw Sheppard being returned to his full self, the aftermath of 'Conversion' was less clear-cut, and Flanigan feels that Sheppard was definitely permanently altered by his experience with the retrovirus. The actor also feels it was a timely reminder of just where the team is in the universe — and that dangers lurk everywhere. "I think that there's a greater capacity for darkness [following 'Conversion'], and an awareness of the real stakes. You can't forget that the stakes are really high. You can be a smart alec all you want, and do your thing, but that's an example of where the stakes really catch him up and remind him that he's as vulnerable as anybody else. I think it definitely changed his character."

Of course, another particularly significant aspect of the season as a whole for the team was the introduction of Ronon Dex, brought in specifically to provide something of a 'sidekick' to Sheppard's necessarily restrained character. The two soldiers developed a firm respect for each other very early on. "I think they just speak the same language," says Flanigan of the relationship between the two characters. "It's primarily gut instinct. I think that Ronon would be essentially [Sheppard's] Id. If he didn't have to sensor himself, he would act pretty much the same way. And I think that likewise, he probably also sees my character as somebody who has the filters he may need, eventually, to harness the impetuousness of just being big and bad," the actor says with a laugh. Å

PROGRESS REPORT
Lieutenant Colonel John Sheppard

I know that many at SGC were dubious about my insistence that John Sheppard be promoted to lieutenant colonel in order to remain as head of military operations in Atlantis. However, the dedication, loyalty and level headedness he showed as a major in Atlantis demonstrated to me that there was only one choice when the question of whether he should be replaced arose. He is a vital part of my team, and despite our previous differences, our second year here in the city has shown how well we work together. Besides all of which, as far as I am concerned, he earned the return of his loyalty through his willingness to sacrifice himself to save the city and everyone in it. I feel that my decision to insist on his promotion has been borne out as the right one by his conduct throughout our second year here in the Pegasus Galaxy. Despite personal trials as a result of the dangers here, Sheppard has still performed his duties to a level I challenge any to match. He was also successful in convincing Ronon Dex, another native to this galaxy with valuable local insight about the Wraith, to join the expedition teams. There is evidence of an inappropriate power struggle still at work between Colonel Sheppard and Colonel Caldwell. However, I believe this abrasive relationship is due to Caldwell's own dissatisfaction with Sheppard's promotion rather than being either instigated by Sheppard or based on a true assessment of his accomplishments. This is perhaps an area that proper discipline and management from SGC could correct.

— **Dr Elizabeth Weir**

DR ELIZABETH WEIR

"If you're asking me whether or not I'm losing sleep over this... Hmm, well, I am taking those sedatives you prescribed."

D r Elizabeth Weir's first year in the city of Atlantis had been tough, and her second would offer the brave diplomat no easy respite. Despite having fooled the Wraith into thinking Atlantis was no more, Weir found herself facing other, equally difficult hardships, alongside some of the most difficult decisions of her career. From personal heartbreak and professional power-struggles to morality issues that would have had Earth's greatest historical philosophers in knots, Weir had plenty to contend with in season two.

"I think she has probably written in her journal a lot of times saying, 'I shouldn't be here. I'm out of my depth and I'm scared and I don't know what I'm doing,'" says actress Torri Higginson. "But I think at the same time she also writes, 'Thank God I'm here, otherwise this would be a completely military base.' What we don't see every week are the other teams that are going on missions, going to other cultures and exchanging drugs and talking and being able to help certain cultures and heal certain people. This other stuff is going on, we're just not seeing it. We're focusing on the perilous activities because that's more dramatic! So I think that on the bad days her journal says, 'I suck, I should leave,' and on the good days she goes, 'Thank God, because otherwise this other stuff wouldn't be done.'"

Despite the trials and tribulations she deals with on a daily basis, Higginson is convinced that Weir still has no regrets about staying on in Atlantis. "I don't know if I would say yes, to begin with, if someone said, 'You have this opportunity to go and work in another galaxy.' I don't know if I could have done that, if I could have left everything I know and gone to a place with a hundred people and maybe never come back. I don't know if my spirit is that curious! But, on a personal level, could you imagine 'real life' for a second if you were asked to do something like that? So for the people that said yes, for them to have that gene in them, that was worth every sacrifice. Now, since she's been there, she's had nothing but more and more amazement. Everything she's come across is something that, three or four years ago, she would have said, 'That's purely fiction.' Now she's finding out that it's science. So I think her heart [is there] now. It would be very difficult to leave."

Weir's determination to remain with the Atlantis team in the Pegasus Galaxy has had plenty of personal ramifications. The events of 'The Intruder' showed that her 'curious spirit' lost her the man she evidently loves, Simon. Higginson believes that despite her heartache, Weir was at least half-expecting Simon to have moved on. "We did an episode in the first year called 'Letters From Pegasus'," she recalls, "where they originally had me writing this long video love-letter to Simon saying, 'I miss you, I love you and I hope everything's good and I can't wait to see you.' I went to Brad [Wright] and said, 'Nobody in this position would do

that to their partner. She has to say, "Don't wait for me, because I have no idea what my future is.'" She didn't expect him to be waiting. She had given him an out, which he had to have, because otherwise it would have been very selfish. I think when she first arrived back it was a surprise for both of them. I think their first message was 'Hey, how are you, are you still around and do you want to see me?' And when it was 'Yes, I do,' and they saw each other, he didn't tell her immediately [about his new life]. So she just assumed that 'Okay, he's still here and he still loves me and there's this great opportunity for him to come back to Atlantis.' At that point she probably would have loved him to do that, because she badly needed a friend."

Weir's loneliness in her position of command was a theme that continued from the show's first year, and was magnified in the second season by the appearance of Mitch Pileggi's character, Colonel Steven Caldwell. Covetous of Sheppard's position and a source of constant conflict for Weir, the doctor found herself under even more pressure. Though Higginson has enjoyed the added potential for friction that Caldwell joining the Atlantis team has created, she still misses Weir and Sheppard butting heads.

"Conflict is always more interesting, and I think it's much more fun to play. Brad said that they were trying to set up Sheppard and Weir to be in that conflict, but they kept just getting web messages saying that the viewers didn't want to see these people at odds. And I had actually been going to Brad and saying that I missed the tête-à-tête with Sheppard, because I think that conflict between people that are friends is more interesting than conflict between adversaries. There's a wonderful 'yo-yo' thing where you can go away and come back [to it] and go away and come back [again]. It's like a fight with someone in the family. It hurts your heart a lot more than a fight with a stranger. So I hope that Caldwell doesn't take that completely, because I think it's interesting to explore the relationship with Weir and Sheppard that way."

Despite the harsh decisions and moralistic quandaries that Weir found herself facing throughout season two, she remained the voice of reason and peace amongst the team. Only once have we seen her wield a gun, and that was while under the influence of an alien entity in 'The Long Goodbye'. Though the actress herself loved the chance to get in on the action , she also appreciates the way that this part of Weir's philosophy has remained constant. "Brad has said that he never wants to see Weir carrying a gun, and I like that he's stuck to that," she says. "That was Brad's idea, and he just kept that straight, which I think is a smart move. There have been times where I've gone, 'Oh no, but I want to, because I want to be on missions and I've got too much time off'... but then they bring me up to shoot with a gun and I'm like, 'Okay, I need my time off again, take the gun back!'" Å

PROGRESS REPORT
Dr Elizabeth Weir

If I am honest, there are times when I am surprised at myself for still being here, for still living in this city. I can't deny that there have been times when I've wanted nothing more than to jump on the *Daedalus* and return to Earth. There was even a time during our return earlier in the year when I considered resigning my post completely, giving up the Pegasus Galaxy permanently and returning home. But I'm glad I didn't. Despite the hardships, despite the difficult decisions and tough issues I have faced in the past year, Atlantis still represents something wondrous to me. It has become a part of me, and I'm not sure that I could give that up now for anything.

In terms of progress over the past year, I am determined to be brutally honest with myself. When I think about what we have achieved, the largest events that loom in my recent memory actually signify failure, not success. We willingly developed the retrovirus, and while our intentions may have been honorable, the outcome was anything but victorious. And now the Earth, which surfaces sometimes in my dreaming moments, is under threat and there is no one to blame but myself. I said yes, I made the decision — I primed the syringe. How can this not now fall on my shoulders? These things crowd out the memories of the good we have done here, the cultures we have helped, what we have learned. And yet, I am determined that the darkest parts of this year will not diminish my faith in this mission.

Atlantis has toughened my resolve. In as much as my time in the Pegasus Galaxy has taught me pragmatism, so too has it taught me that we are more resilient as a race than we sometimes credit ourselves. We will prevail, we will succeed. And I, for one, will have learned.

— **Dr Elizabeth Weir**

DR RODNEY MCKAY

"I'm not crazy. I just have another consciousness in my brain."

Having proved himself a true genius (and one that certainly knows it) countless time throughout *Stargate: Atlantis'* first season, there was really only one way Rodney McKay could go in season two — down. The crash came early on in the year, as 'Trinity' proved that there were some things not even McKay could fix, and as far as actor David Hewlett is concerned, that, in some ways at least, overshadowed the rest of the character's year.

"There's definitely insecurity," says Hewlett of the character in season two. "He's always insecure — I suppose that's where a lot of his 'snarkasm' comes from — but I think season two definitely shook him. You've got things like 'Trinity', where he makes mistakes, he thinks he's smarter than he is. Although," says the actor with a chuckle, "I think there was still something wrong with the machinery... So there's definitely some stuff where McKay finds that he is in fact fallible."

For Hewlett, having McKay fail has only added to the character. "There's nothing worse than a character that turns up and says, 'Oh, well you turn this and everything will be fine.' It's the fact that you don't know who's going to mess up this time. So that was nice, because it added this great kind of dynamic, especially with Joe [Flanigan]'s character, where he's now always asking McKay, 'Are you *sure*?' All of a sudden he's got a few digs that wouldn't have worked in season one."

Despite suffering such a setback, according to Hewlett, McKay didn't change either his outlook or his attitude in the aftermath of 'Trinity'. "The funny thing is," laughs the actor, "I don't know that he does learn from it. I joke about the fact that there was something wrong, that it was out of his control, but the reality is, if he did have a little bit more time, maybe he *could* have worked it out. That's the nature of science and discovery. You have to push things, and sometimes things go wrong. You learn. He won't make that mistake again, but I think he's certainly going to make those types of mistakes again. He can't help it!"

McKay's loud-mouthing often covers a genuine anxiety about his safety, which, let's face it, isn't particularly surprising given his background as a non-military scientist and the constant peril in which the team finds themselves. Fear is a perfectly reasonable response under the circumstances, and Hewlett never wants the doctor to forget that. "The thing that I don't want to forget, and I don't want him to forget, is the fact that we don't know what's going to happen next. It's like being on a mission that never ends. There is never a sense of 'Phew!' We're *still* on a foreign planet, we're *still* dealing with technology that's way beyond us. We have the ability to go home, but we're not able to. In time, that's also addictive. What's McKay got to go home to? 'No new message'... I think he lives for this, [although] he had a different sense of what it was going to be like. He doesn't like going outdoors. He likes work-

DR RODNEY MCKAY

ing things out. He's not a big fan of actually having to physically do anything. And it's important, that's sort of McKay's role... I personify everyone's fear," Hewlett laughs, "that little part of everyone of us that's absolutely terrified and doesn't do the right thing at the right time. In fact, who often does the *wrong* thing. I still don't know why they give him guns!"

Since the original team from Earth has now been living in Atlantis together for a year, it may come as a surprise that Hewlett doesn't feel that McKay's relationships with his fellow workers have become any more settled — in fact, he feels the opposite is true. "I think, strangely, they are less comfortable," the actor reveals. "Having worked together for as long as they have, he's pissed everybody off, including himself. The neat thing I found was, in 'Trinity', which is just five or six episodes in, he makes that big mistake, and he spends the rest of the season paying for that, really. He's questioned, he's insecure about certain stuff, he's the butt of a number of jokes because of it. He's also made friendly with the military when he's needed to, and that puts him at odds with Weir. So I think if there's anyone with which there's a growing relationship, it's probably between him and Ronon. Because Ronon is what McKay would love to be. Strong, good looking and always doing the right thing, instead of the little guy in the back going, 'Um, excuse me?!' And it's a great dynamic. It's the same thing with Joe's character, too. Sheppard is the cool guy who knows just enough science to get by and enough of the technology to get by. But I think in a funny way, [Ronon] is the 'oil' in the vinegar salad dressing that is season two! I think separation is fun, as opposed to bonding. Which is neat because then at the end of season two there is that kind of cohesion with all the characters trying to work as a team, as opposed to working against each other."

Though the year has been less than comfortable for McKay, Hewlett has continued to have great fun playing the character, and identifies one episode as a particular high point in the season. "Definitely 'Grace Under Pressure'," he says enthusiastically of the episode where McKay was reunited with *Stargate SG-1*'s Samantha Carter (Amanda Tapping). "I love that connection back *to Stargate SG-1*, because it's like going home. That's where it all started, and it's just so nice to work with Amanda again, and to work in water, which is surprisingly fun," he laughs. "It's like taking a bath all day! And then of course 'Duet'. Those are shows that actors long to get, because there are shows where there's lots of stuff going on for everybody — which I generally think are the best episodes, where everybody's got something going on — but as an actor you can't help but love those episodes where you go, 'Oh! Look! I get to play.' And 'Grace Under Pressure' and 'Duet' are two [of those] that really stand out." Å

PROGRESS REPORT
Dr Rodney McKay

It's been a difficult year for all of us, but I believe Rodney McKay has found it the most testing. His unwavering confidence in his own abilities proved to be flawed during his attempts to reactivate the Ancient weapons battery found during a recon mission to the Dorandan home world. To be honest, I was concerned that this set-back would cause problems for the running of Atlantis, not only from the point of view of McKay's confidence suffering, but also in regards to the blind faith that he often expects from his colleagues.

Although the latter has continued to be a cause for concern (I think that Rodney knows he has to earn that faith back over time), I needn't have worried about his confidence. McKay still exhibits that same passion, enthusiasm, brilliance and, though I hesitate to acknowledge it, arrogance, that made him such an attractive proposition as a member of the Atlantis team in the first place.

I still have concerns about how he integrates into the team personally — none of us have had much time for recreation, but I do worry that McKay takes no time at all to relax, or to build the relationships that are so important to the workings of a team like ours. But, as his professional contributions to the workings of Atlantis have been, as usual, faultless since that early incident, I cannot take this as a cause for complaint. Rodney McKay, as volatile as he is, is an extremely valuable member of this team, and I would not want to be here in the Pegasus Galaxy without him.

— **Dr Elizabeth Weir**

DR CARSON BECKETT

"I feel not unlike the priest in *The Exorcist.*"

For both actor Paul McGillion and his ever more intrepid character Dr Carson Beckett, *Stargate: Atlantis'* second year signified a distinct change. Though originally planned as only a recurring character, McGillion's portrayal of the nervous Beckett had proven so popular that the producers invited him to take his place as a regular cast member for the show's second year.

"I was in almost every episode," the actor smiles, discussing how the change manifested itself throughout season two. "There's a few that I wasn't in, 'The Lost Boys', 'Aurora' and 'Grace Under Pressure', but the ones I was in were fantastic. Beckett had a nice opportunity to go off-world, which was fantastic, and made for some interesting comedy as well."

Besides being made a regular, Carson Beckett found himself at the center of the season's most compelling storyline. The retrovirus Beckett develops could prove the end of the Pegasus Galaxy's Wraith problem, if only the Atlantis team can overcome the disturbing moral question it raises... "The retrovirus became a really interesting plotline throughout the whole season, and Beckett is heavily involved in that. The second half of the season becomes an interesting moralistic dilemma for Beckett. You're really dealing with bio-ethics. What are our limitations? What should we do and what should we not do? He goes into a bit of a dark place for the second half of the season."

This "dark place" is something of a change for the doctor. In the first season, viewers had often seen him providing a foil in McKay's most humorous moments, as well as offering 'light relief' himself through his continual fear of the alien situation he found himself in within Atlantis. McGillion himself welcomes the chance to deepen the character, while voicing a desire that Beckett maintain a healthy balance between comedy and drama. "He's been torn in many different ways this season. You do get the comedic episodes, which is great and which I really enjoy. You get those moments, but on the other side of the spectrum you get really heavy and dramatic scenes with Beckett, too. Like anyone's history, all of these things become a part of who you are. It may harden the character to a certain degree, but I don't think Beckett will ever lose his sense of humor and his [gentler] sensibility. At the end of the day he knows he's doing a job and he may be hard on himself but not to the degree where it's going to affect him. A lot of that is obviously up to the writers and the way they streamline Beckett, but I don't think they'll lose that charm and that sensibility, because I think that's really important for the character to keep. As an actor I always try to instill it, and they're open to ideas, suggestions and concerns. But I don't think it's so much him going dark or maniacal, it's that the situation he's put in is very dark. You know, it's a moral dilemma, and when anybody faces a moral dilemma, it's a tough place to be in. Unfortunately, he has to deal with it. I like it for the character, because it puts him in a place where, I think, people might empathize with his dilemma."

DR CARSON BECKETT

When asked to discuss the most significant episodes for Beckett in season two, it seems that picking a favorite is a difficult task for McGillion: "From the top, I liked what I had to do in 'The Siege III' — I thought that was fantastic. My favorite episode of the season was 'Duet' because I love acting with David Hewlett. 'Duet', in many ways, is a 'David episode', but the combination of both of us together, where I play the straight man, makes for good comic timing and good humor. I really enjoyed that episode a lot. 'Instinct' and 'Conversion' are two very heavy Beckett episodes — he gets into some interesting dilemmas when he goes off-world, as well as still being the doctor that he is and caring fellow that he is. 'Michael' is a heavy Beckett episode, and 'Allies' is a great Beckett episode as well. With 'Michael', I thought, 'Wow, this is a really dark episode, yet very interesting as well,' and I like playing that. When there's a struggle for the character I find that the most interesting for me as an actor."

McGillion's enthusiasm for Beckett is reflected in his dedication to the character. Not only has he worked to perfect the Scots accent — which after two years has become accurate enough to please even the actor's Scottish relatives — but McGillion is also determined to deliver the doctor's medical terminology convincingly. "It's fun to come and play this character all the time. It's such a departure for me in so many ways, and an homage to my heritage, [which] is great. I just become more and more comfortable with the accent all the time. I think it's really become more solid. I have some relatives who watch the show quite a bit in Scotland who phone me up and say, 'Oh your accent's just perfect this year.' And they'd be the first ones to tell you that you were a bit dodgy at the start! I talk in my Scottish accent to my parents all the time. I don't even think about the accent. I make sure, especially when I'm dealing with medical jargon, that I can say certain words with a Scottish accent. My brother's doing his PHG in Medicine, and I'll call him up and do the line to him. I've had some crazy lines!"

Not that the hard work is a problem as far as McGillion is concerned — it's all part of the job. "You've just got to do the work," he shrugs. "I want to work hard. I want to make sure I come across as believable, and honor the text. For that to happen, you just have to put the time in. I come home as soon as I finish on set and I just start memorizing again. I work hard on the weekends and, on Sundays, I put aside four hours to just go over the script for the week. Friends of mine read the lines with me and it's just back and fourth non-stop so I make sure I get it down. I just want to digest it so it's in the body. I don't want to be looking for lines while I'm on set. That's something I really pride myself in. I know also that time is money and I want to make sure I'm on my game, that I can come in and deliver the goods. Of course sometimes you're going to slip up, but I try not to." Å

PROGRESS REPORT
Dr Carson Beckett

Few of my team have conducted themselves in quite such an outstanding way over the past year as Dr Beckett. Though it would have been understandable for him to have suffered anxiety following the events preceding the cloaking of Atlantis at the beginning of the year, the city's doctor has never shied away from the tasks before him. Some of them, I am quite sure, would have stumped even the most brilliant minds in medicine back on Earth. Take, for instance, the way in which he handled Rodney McKay's affliction after he deliberately took a dose of Wraith enzyme. I am convinced that it was only Beckett's unique experience, developed whilst in the Pegasus Galaxy, that allowed him to find a way of weaning McKay from the drug. And I know that the fact that he was not able to do the same for Lieutenant Ford has weighed heavily upon him.

If anything, Beckett's conscience — which, to my mind, is the most valuable tool a member of our expedition can possess — is what has made the past few months so difficult for him. Having developed the idea of the retrovirus — which I know for a fact came from a positive desire to create a peaceful solution to the Wraith 'problem' — I know that his conscience has been troubled once again. It's a sentiment I can and do sympathize with whole-heartedly, and as I look at where this serum could possibly take us, I wonder what it is going to do to its inventor. This is a situation I intend to monitor closely, and although I trust Carson implicitly, I have recommended that he talk to Dr Heightmeyer. It can only help. Meanwhile, he continues to perform his duties with impeccable dedication. I am grateful that he has remained with us here — I would not want to trust the health and wellbeing of my team to any other doctor.

— **Dr Elizabeth Weir**

TEYLA EMMAGAN

"Establishing good relations with our neighbors is not just about trade."

T he renewal of *Stargate: Atlantis* for a second season was a welcome surprise for Rachel Luttrell, who had from the outset prepared herself for the worst. After all, successful television shows are few and far between, and of the plethora of new shows launched every year, those that are cancelled far outweigh those that run.

"It was just exciting to come back," the actress explains. "In the first season, I kind of imagined that I'd be up in Vancouver for maybe six months, and shoot this show and then head back to Los Angeles. So it was a tremendous feeling to be coming back for the next season! We connected more as actors and as people, and certainly as characters as well."

For Luttrell, one of the most significant aspects of season two was the introduction of Jason Momoa, the new regular cast member, who would be appearing as Ronon Dex. "I think the biggest thing that stands out for me from season two is our new cast member," says Luttrell with a laugh. "Getting Jason on board meant our dynamic shifted a little bit. All of a sudden we had another warrior, and that was very cool, very interesting. I remember the very first time that he showed up on set. I had met him in the make-up trailer, and bumped into David [Hewlett] on the way to my trailer and David said, 'So what do you think, what's he like?'" She laughs, "Everybody was nervous, because we weren't sure whether or not he would fit into our little group that we had cultivated so wonderfully in the first season. But it all worked out fantastically well. He's definitely part of the family."

This shift in dynamic on set was echoed on screen as Ronon appeared in Atlantis and became a valued part of Sheppard's team. As one of his earliest acquaintances in the city and with a similar background, Teyla was among the first to get to know the young warrior, and their bond continued to grow throughout the second season. "I think it's made her more comfortable, in a way," says the actress of Ronon's influence on Teyla. "Now there's a member of the team that shares part of her perspective, who has a similar background in terms of where they both came from and what they had to deal with growing up, with reference points to the Wraith. And certainly, having someone else on board who is a warrior, somebody who has battled and run from the Wraith for so long, it's given her a very unique ally on the team. She doesn't feel as much of an outcast — not that she necessarily did, but now there's somebody else there who really shares her perspective, and I think that's really cool.

Even with a new ally to empathize to some degree with her situation, for the only Athosian on the intrepid Atlantis team, the second year in the city of the ancestors would bring many challenges. Teyla's year became progressively more difficult emotionally, particularly with the loss of a loved one in 'Critical Mass', and new experiences of the Wraith in episodes such as 'Instinct' and 'Michael'.

For Luttrell, Teyla's response as she was forced to consider the Wraith in a new light in

TEYLA EMMAGAN

'Michael' is a measure of her personal strength. "I loved 'Michael' in particular, and I thought it was a wonderful turning point, specifically for Teyla. Just being faced with the human side of the Wraith and actually feeling a connection to this character that we decided to call Michael — and I really do think that they shared quite a connection. Teyla was against the whole retrovirus to begin with. She was against the whole tampering with genes and what that would mean moralistically and what that would mean in terms of her notion of the Wraith. It really shifted things for her, not necessarily in terms of how she looked at the Wraith, because they're still an awful, evil creature, but in terms of just, 'How much right do we have to tamper with another creature, whether or not we agree with their being alive?' There's a line right at the very end of 'Michael', where she looks at him as he's starting to change and she says, 'You and I will no longer be friends.' And that was very interesting that she would even consider that they *were* friends. That was a very fun episode for me to shoot, because I think Connor and I worked together really well."

Teyla's connection with the Wraith as a whole was another aspect of the character that expanded from season one to become a feature of season two. Though she was able to use this power to help save the city in 'The Siege III', it remains to be seen whether the fact that Teyla has Wraith DNA will be a blessing or a curse for both herself and those around her still battling the enemy. "The fact that she shares some DNA with them is very interesting," agrees Luttrell. "It's not clear, but there's something brewing there. The DNA and what that means for her definitely needs to be explored. It's who she is, and at this point none of us really know how far-reaching that will be, but I think it's something that could be a cornerstone, certainly of who Teyla's character is and perhaps even of the storyline. Already we are seeing Teyla making use of those skills, and hopefully we'll get to deepen that and her understanding of it, because it's something that's new to her."

There are several other aspects of the character that Luttrell looks forward to pursuing, particularly the idea of seeing more of Teyla's personal life. "I'm interested in exploring Teyla's past," the actress explains. "That would be fascinating — how did she become the leader of her people, what were the dynamics with her family, and are there any family members still out there somewhere? There is a whole wealth of backstory there that I would love to get an opportunity to explore. I would also like to explore some romance for Teyla." Of course, season two did touch on the idea that something of the sort could grow between Teyla and Sheppard, but Luttrell is less sure what path a romantic interlude for her character could take. She laughs when asked who she has in mind for the job of Teyla's love interest. "No one in particular! It could come from an incredibly surprising place. It could come from a place that we don't know and haven't visited. I don't know, but I would like that opportunity. I think that would be an interesting way of exploring another side of who she is." Å

PROGRESS REPORT
Teyla Emmagan

Throughout the course of our second year in the Pegasus Galaxy, Teyla has continued to show our team an unrivalled level of loyalty, and once again we are in her debt. Her unique perspective on life in this place, coupled with a voice of reason that belies her youth, has constantly provided me with valuable information and valued opinions that I would not otherwise have available to me. Through Teyla, we have experienced some of the best things about this galaxy — people and places that her local knowledge alone has allowed us to find.

Her loyalty has, this year, occasionally been at the expense of her own better judgment. This has particularly been the case with regards to our dealings with the Wraith over the past few months. Teyla, of all of us, understands what it means to live in fear of the Wraith, and her sensibilities on the subject have been pushed to the limit by events. Despite her misgivings about using the retrovirus, she has been able to put aside her personal feelings and assist us with what we have most needed.

Teyla has also been able to help with the integration of Atlantis' most recently-arrived resident, Ronon Dex. I must confess that at first, when Sheppard voiced his desire to add Ronon to his regular mission team, I was more than dubious. My own encounters with him have been, to date, very brief and somewhat uncomfortable. Teyla, however, has taken Ronon under her wing, and as a result I have seen him become more and more a part of our community here in Atlantis. On Earth, she would make an excellent teacher or diplomat — here in Atlantis, she is an invaluable member of our team.

— **Dr Elizabeth Weir**

RONON DEX

"I was beginning to think you were afraid to fight."

The evolution of a new character starts long before the cameras role on their first episode. For Jason Momoa, an actor formerly known for his roles in *North Shore* and *Baywatch: Hawaii*, the morning of his initial *Atlantis* audition is fixed in his mind for a rather unusual reason! "I ended up having a gas leak at my house that night, [before] going to the audition," he recalls. "We were sucking in gas for eight hours! We had a three-storey house and my roommate came out from the top floor and said, 'I can smell something weird,' and I didn't know what was going on. So I was going to the audition [having] had nine hours of toxic gas intake, I was blacking in and out…"

After being checked out by the emergency services, Momoa bravely carried on with reading in the audition. "Getting there, I met Joe [Flanigan]. It's always a little strange — you have to stand in front of a big table, with about fifteen people behind it," he says of the audition process. "That keeps the nerves going! I think they gave me 'Runner' to read, and they decided I was perfect for the role — someone in dreads, six-foot-four… They were looking for a soldier, they wanted someone who looked a little primitive."

Securing the role of Satedan 'Specialist' Ronon Dex was only the first of a range of obstacles Momoa faced before becoming settled in as a regular member of the *Stargate: Atlantis* cast. First of all, he had to relocate from Los Angeles to Vancouver at fairly short notice, having just returned to the States from Australia. Also, since the rest of the actors had already been filming for a full year before Momoa's character was introduced, integrating could have been difficult, a fact of which the actor was well aware, and understandably a little apprehensive about. "Every show I've done, I've come in on the first episode [of the] season, and it's been a new show," he explains. "So it was a bit weird, but everyone was so cool. I just fit right in."

In a mirror of the actor's own integration into *Stargate: Atlantis*, Ronon's first few episodes as part of the Atlantis team were all about adjusting to life in the city of the Ancients. Having been alone and on the run for so long, suddenly finding himself surrounded by the inhabitants of Atlantis was something of a shock to the system for the young warrior, whose instincts are often to attack first and ask questions later.

"He's perfectly alright being on the outside," explains Momoa. "Several times, his way of thinking has been obviously totally different to the team on Atlantis, but sometimes he'll agree. I don't want that to ever change. I don't want him to lose that edge that he has. Also the Atlantis team trust him in those moments. He'll hold back for so long, and then they'll say, 'Yeah, do it.' So you need that, and I enjoy having the 'rogue warrior' element to him. From where I am right now, he's fully relaxed. But his hatred of the Wraith is one thing that will never fade. He'll never ever forget. When he's in trouble he'll never pull back. I tried to do it in one episode. He is trying to change his whole level of thinking. He's questioning someone and he's just like… he's changing what he does because his normal action would be

to just react, straight to action. And I think it's good for him to have that battle going on inside. So he tries to conform to their ways a bit, but not too much."

Dex has nevertheless found friends in Atlantis, particularly in the form of the team's other 'alien' resident, Teyla Emmagan. Their relationship has developed into something of a big sister-little brother scenario, with Teyla, the calmer, more cautious fighter, taking the lead and reeling Ronon in during his wilder moments. "I'm glad it's developed that way," say Momoa. "Teyla doesn't come from my planet, but it's someone I trust and can confide in. And there are a lot of things I've given up to Teyla. I really enjoy our relationship on the show."

For Momoa, there were several highlights to his first year on the show. One of them was 'Trinity', in which Ronon realizes that he may not be the last of his race in the universe after all. "I think the one [moment] between Teyla and I, when I say that the whole of the planet and the people I love have gone, it's a huge thing," says Momoa. "Everything you love is gone, and for seven years I've been hunted. Just that moment that you discover there's someone out there, and that there may be a lot [of others] out there. And also, living like the character is in 'Runner' — that way of not talking to anyone, of not being able to stop anywhere. You just kind of get into that mind set. It was amazing. I just became part of the team after 'Duet', going on certain missions, but 'Trinity' was really interesting."

Momoa is excited about the prospect of exploring the character in greater depth, and reports that while he is satisfied with everything he had to do in season two, there is still much more he wants to address. "The whole season was pretty mapped out before I got here," the actor explains, "so you come and do your job, and it's exciting. This is my job, I'm an actor, to come in and look forward to the next script, to read it and make suggestions over a period of time. Right now I'm extremely happy with what I'm playing. But [I'd love] more relationship things. It's a team thing, every once in a while you get to focus on a certain character. And I've had two great episodes for that. There are things that we haven't really established, so it could be really fun and interesting to see what happens. It would be nice to develop the backstory. There's a lot of things that I would like to incorporate about what my past was."

Momoa would also like a chance to work with different members of the cast, and has one in particular in mind. "I guess the one [relationship] that I haven't explored a lot is with Beckett," the actor says thoughtfully. "I love Paul [McGillion], he's a favorite, so to work with him more would be nice — just to get him off planet, because I'm always off-world and he's always back at the base. I actually had a scene with Mitch [Pileggi] the other day, and for the first time he says, 'Thank you for saving my life.' So it would be good to work with Caldwell more. But other than that I think I'm pretty well rounded, really." Å

PROGRESS REPORT
Ronan Dex

Although Ronon is not officially a member of our team, as with Teyla Emmagan, I feel it appropriate to update SGC with news of his progress over the course of the year. Among all the things that happened in Atlantis this year, adding another member to our team was one of the most unexpected, and I will admit, when Sheppard first brought Dex back to the city from the planet where he found him, I would not have welcomed him staying more than a few days. Seven years of being on the run from the Wraith, near-starving and in a constant state of readiness for combat had left him angry, isolated and unapproachable. Though sympathetic to the reasons why, I at first thought that Ronon's understand-ably abrasive personality would mean he would find it impossible to adapt to our ways of working. My own attempts at communication with the young man weren't the resounding success I would have liked them to be.

Nevertheless, Colonel Sheppard's insistence that Ronon be made a part of his team was evidently the right choice. Though still a little rough around the edges — as I personally think he always will, and possibly should, be — Ronon has worked hard in his own way to fit in with his team and our wider community. It is a testament to the dedication of both John Sheppard and Teyla that he has remained with us, and has become such an intrinsic part of life in Atlantis. His bravery, ingenuity and sheer tenacity have proved a valuable asset for Sheppard in the field, and it would be true to say that were he to leave us now, Earth would lose an important part of their Atlantis task force.

— **Dr Elizabeth Weir**

COLONEL STEVEN CALDWELL

"We don't have time to debate morality. Unfortunately, sometimes you have to do unpleasant things to save lives."

The first new face to appear in *Stargate: Atlantis'* second season was veteran genre actor Mitch Pileggi, in the stern military role of Colonel Steven Caldwell, commander of the battleship *Daedalus*. No stranger either to science fiction or filming in Vancouver, BC, Pileggi is best known for his role of Walter Skinner in *The X-Files*. Clearly, he's an actor who knows a winning show when he sees one! Still, Pileggi admits to the usual nerves when joining a show, particularly one with a cast that had already been well-established for a year. "Sometimes it's [difficult], sometimes it isn't, and this was one of those situations where it wasn't," he recalls. "I felt almost immediately like I had been there for a long time, working with these people. They took me into the fold and it's been such a pleasure to work with them. The fact that some of the crew working on the show were people I had worked with before was really a pleasant experience, too. I just remember how receptive they were about a new guy coming onto the set. That's always important to an actor."

As a character, Caldwell had been introduced to shake things up a little, disturbing Weir and Sheppard's insular, isolated world in the Pegasus Galaxy, and that was certainly something he managed to do. Despite his differences with various members of the Atlantis crew, however, Caldwell swiftly established himself as a valuable member of the team.

"I liked the interactions with the characters," Pileggi says. "There were times that Caldwell and Weir would go at it, and there were times that they were more civilized with each other, and the same with some of the other characters. One of my favorite episodes was 'The Long Goodbye', where I get to really interact with Dr McKay a lot. They were like two kids when the Mom and Dad were gone, just letting go at each other," the actor laughs. "It was Sheppard and Weir being taken over by these alien entities, and we were left to try to straighten things out, and keep everything from completely falling apart. Just the chaos that ensued in that situation was interesting, and a lot of fun to play."

Another episode from season two sticks in Pileggi's mind for an entirely unexpected reason — 'Critical Mass', in which Caldwell is discovered to be hosting a Goa'uld parasite intent on destroying the city. "What I remember most about that episode is Jason Momoa throwing me against the wall and (almost) breaking my back!" Pileggi says with a wry laugh. "He's a big boy, he's strong, and I wasn't expecting it! I can still feel my head rattling on that wall he threw me against. It was kind of jarring. Fortunately we only had to do a couple of takes. But once was enough! The second one I was like, 'Jason, don't throw me so hard! This body isn't as young as it used to be!' But he was great to work with. I can't say that that part of it was fun, but it turned out fine!"

As the commander of the *Daedalus*, much of Caldwell's time is spent on the bridge of that great ship, traveling between Earth and Atlantis, lending a hand to defend the city, or taking the team on exploratory missions such as in the episode 'Aurora'. It's an arrangement that Pileggi enjoys, for the most part, although he would love the chance to get Caldwell out in the field at least once or twice. "I liked a lot of the time that I was on the ship set, all the battle sequences and so forth. Sometimes they were tough to shoot, but always fun. They've taken him in a fair number of directions. It would be fun to go out and go through one of the gates with them sometime and play out in the field with them. I don't know if there's a possibility for that to happen, but I think it would be kind of cool to go off-world with them at some point and just get outside, slip around in the mud! I think more than anything he was a pilot, always flying, so I don't know if he's had a lot of opportunity for that type of stuff. It would be cool to go out [in an F-302] and shoot a few of the darts down. But a lot of times the ship has been battered in a battle and they have to take it back and repairs have to be made, so I do get to go to Atlantis and hang out."

Having enjoyed his visit to the Pegasus Galaxy during season two, Pileggi knows where he would like to take the Caldwell character next. "I'd love to do a crossover on *Stargate SG-1*," he says. "I'd love to work with Amanda [Tapping] again. She came to the set recently and it was the first time I had seen her since I started working on the show because she was gone a lot with the baby. I worked with her years ago on *The X-Files*. I'd love to have the opportunity to work with some of the other folks over there." Å

PROGRESS REPORT
Colonel Steven Caldwell

Though not a permanent member of the team here in Atlantis, and not answerable to me in my capacity as civilian leader, I thought it important to include a report on Colonel Caldwell and his past year of involvement with the city's inhabitants.

I think, unfortunately, my own relationship with the colonel was destined to be difficult right from the start, due to my insistence that John Sheppard remain as the military head of operations in Atlantis and the fact that Caldwell desired that command position himself. As a result, despite my best efforts, our relationship has been at best strained and at worst antagonistic. I understand that Caldwell has the experience, and also enjoys the backing of SGC thanks to his past military record, but for my part, John Sheppard's knowledge of the Pegasus Galaxy and the way he has conducted himself since he agreed to join this expedition has given him the right to remain in the position that he now enjoys. Though having the *Daedalus* available to the city has provided us with a

measure of security that we previously did not have, Caldwell's clear desire to take command of the military operation here in Atlantis has often made the ship's presence uncomfortable. He has used every opportunity to implement his own method of working, including immediately changing the security operation when he was temporarily charged with Sheppard's duties. In short, I do not feel that Caldwell respects me or the work that our team has accomplished in the Pegasus Galaxy. I feel that were I not here, the military would completely oust the original civilian ideals of this expedition. It remains to be seen how much longer we can continue working together in such an atmosphere.

— **Dr Elizabeth Weir.**

RECURRING CAST

"It doesn't feel very healthy in here..."
— Lieutenant Laura Cadman

*S*targate: Atlantis' second year introduced a new set of faces, not only in the regular and semi-regular cast line-up, but also in its recurring cast members. With the arrival of the *Daedalus* and a new ZPM, Atlantis had the opportunity to replenish its task force from Earth, and with the change of personnel came Major Lorne, played by **Kavan Smith**. Appearing in eight episodes of the show's second season, Lorne soon became an indispensable member of Sheppard's team, acting as his right-hand man when the newly-promoted Lieutenant Colonel was away.

Below: Smith as Major Lorne in 'Condemned'.

Canadian-born Smith is a native of Vancouver, and has appeared in various genre shows including *The 4400*. He had also previously appeared in *Stargate SG-1*'s seventh season, playing a Major called Lawrence in 'Enemy Mine'. When the call went out for a new recurring character on *Stargate: Atlantis*, Smith was happy to audition. "I went in just thinking that perhaps they would bring back the character," the actor recalls. "They said, 'Oh yeah, that's perfect, we'll just bring back the old character.'" In fact, the character got renamed Lorne and was given more of a military stance than the scientific leanings of Lawrence, but Smith is still more than happy to be appearing as a semi-regular on the show.

"I think my favorite moment as far as shooting and probably as far as the character development goes is without a doubt 'Runner'," he says. "I had a lot of really good stuff to do with David [Hewlett]. 'Conversion' was also a lot of fun. That was a lot of, on set, really neat stuff with the caves and then with all the CGI stuff — it was a lot of fun. But, as an actor, 'Runner' definitely stands out."

It looked for a time as if Major Lorne's life in Atlantis would be cut short, with the events of 'Coup D'Etat' suggesting the character's early demise. Happily, however, that turned out not to be the case. "I was surprised — the script said that my character was found dead. I thought, 'Ok, I guess I ended up in a *Star Trek* red shirt. I'm gone!' But then we found out, of course, that I did not in fact die. I was told by the director at the time that they had plans for my character… So I think Lorne might be around [for a while], but in what capacity I don't really know."

Lieutenant Laura Cadman was another new recruit to arrive in Atlantis via the *Daedalus*. Played by young American actress **Jaime Ray Newman**, the character provided a new sparring partner for Dr Rodney McKay (as if he needed any more), and a possible budding love interest for Dr Carson Beckett. Feisty, capable and smart enough to keep up with McKay, Cadman's first adventure alongside Sheppard's team led her to end up a little too close to the good doctor for comfort — in his head, no less! She survived that ordeal well enough, and managed to telegraph her interest in Beckett in a most unusual way. More trouble was to come, however. Her second appearance, much later in the year, for 'Critical Mass', once again saw her teamed with McKay, not quite as a partnership but still with plenty of opportunities for her to be the butt of McKay's trademark 'snarkasm', as he became increasingly suspicious of her motivations for being in Atlantis.

Below: Newman as Lieutenant Laura Cadman with her sparring partner, McKay.

Born in Michigan, talented Newman has many feathers in her performing cap. Starting life as a jazz singer before turning to acting, she landed her first acting role on popular long-running American soap *General Hospital*, but not before she had formed her own stage production company and produced three plays over just two years. Despite moving to Los Angeles to pursue acting as a main career, Newman still sings regularly around the city in her band Schoolboy Crush.

Below: Frizzell in one of her Wraith Queen guises, in 'Allies'.

Though most viewers won't be aware of it, they have been watching actress **Andee Frizzell** in *Stargate: Atlantis* since the very first episode, 'Rising'. Frizzell has been buried under a ton of make-up for each of the different roles she has performed on the show, bringing to life the terrifying varieties of Wraith Queens the Atlantis team has had to confront during their years in the Pegasus Galaxy. Each of the characters has looked and sounded completely different, and that it's the same actress behind them all is a testament to Frizzell's talent. That she gives each Wraith Queen her own personality and manner is all the more astonishing given the full-head prosthetics Frizzell wears (which includes contact lenses that restrict the performer's vision and a whole slew of different wigs). The actress, who lives and works in Vancouver, BC, has also worked on television shows such as *Gene Roddenberry's Andromeda* and independent movies such as *Devour*. Since Frizzell has proved herself so capable in the guise of the Wraith, viewers are sure to see the actress many times yet — no matter how many Wraith Queens the Atlantis team manage to defeat!

One face that viewers had already got used to seeing around the corridors of Atlantis during season one was Dr Radek Zelenka, a Czech scientist who countless times proved himself equal to McKay's demands. The actor behind the character, **David Nykl**, made such an impression on the producers during season one that they brought him back for the second year. Thus,

Zelenka became a permanent 'fixture' in the city of Atlantis, and found himself participating in some of the biggest missions he had faced so far — including going off-world for the first time in 'Duet'. "He's grown from just being a recurring character, and now I've got the opportunity to do some significant things in the show and deal with some important plot points," Nykl agrees enthusiastically.

For the actor, the season yielded several high points in a year packed with important plot lines and ongoing dramas. "'Grace Under Pressure', that was really fun," enthuses Nykl, "because I had a whole episode basically with Joe [Flanigan]. I really enjoyed 'Duet' as well, that was a lot of fun to do. And other than that, there have been little bits for Zelenka throughout. I liked 'Critical Mass', when I get sent off to deal with the children," he laughs. "It was quite funny! I would like the chance to be able to do some more each year, but I think the show will be around for a while yet! So I hope to be a part of it." Å

Above: Nykl as Dr Radek Zelenka.

PETER BODNARUS

Ⓐll of *Stargate: Atlantis'* design elements — from the beautifully rendered physical sets to the computer-generated features such as the city of Atlantis herself — begin life on the desks of the production's art department. Neither *Stargate SG-1* nor *Stargate: Atlantis* could ever be accused of doing things by halves, and as if to prove it, the producers decided to bring in an entirely new CG element for season two in the shape of Atlantis' very own warship. Thus, for the show's second year on air, illustrator Peter Bodnarus found himself charged with developing a new version of *Stargate SG-1's* biggest warship, the *Prometheus.*

"My main contribution for the beginning of the season was designing the *Daedalus* inside and out," Bodnarus explains. "Basically, I start off by getting direction from [production designer] Bridget McGuire as to what her vision is for the particular set that I'll be designing. Bridget tends to give me a lot of freedom around designing technology. It seems to be something I have a good instinct for. I used to be an architect and my dream as a boy was to be an industrial designer. I've always had a love of the way technology looks, and I bring a lot of that into the work I do."

Such a background certainly came in useful for designing the *Daedalus*, which, as an evolution of the *Prometheus*, demanded a certain look that deliberately emulated military designs existing in the real world. "For the *Daedalus*, we started with the existing *Prometheus* set. The idea was that we were building on this existing technology, sort of refitting the older ship to build a new space ship. A lot of the systems are building on what was previously there. So I started with exploring a new look for the systems console. I did a bunch of sketches of possible new levels and new types of interactivity for the set. Then we [produced] a really distinctive feature that would make this very different from the *Prometheus*, a new forward window. Bridget had actually done a very quick sketch on a post-it note, and had given that to me and said, 'Do something with that.' So from that I created a sketch and I showed that to her and she said, 'That's the direction to go.'"

Though many of these elements

Below: One of Bodnarus' designs for the *Daedalus'* interior.

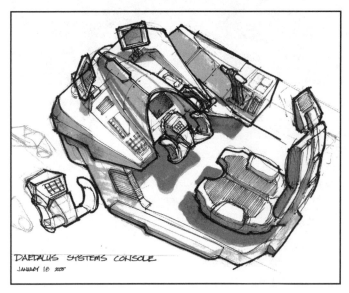

DAEDALUS SYSTEMS CONSOLE
JANUARY 18 2005

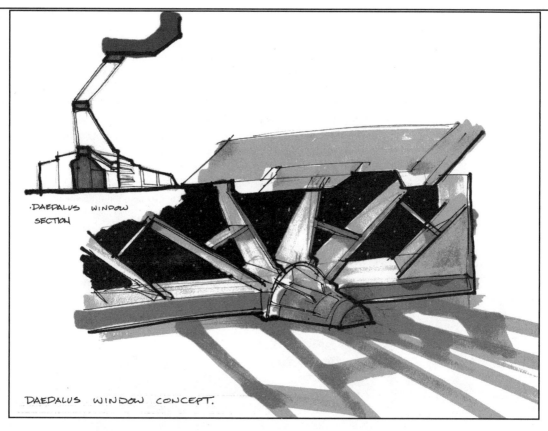

·DAEDALUS WINDOW
SECTION

DAEDALUS WINDOW CONCEPT.

start life with a very simple pen-and-pencil sketch, the artist knows that they will eventually be rendered in a computer-generated environment. This being the case, Bodnarus often uses a computer medium to fill out his designs beyond the initial sketch stage. "A lot of the stuff I build in the computer first — I'll actually build a real 3-D virtual model of the set, and if everything's working in cyberspace then [I know] it'll work. It's analogous to building a cardboard model. Then I take pictures of it, and you can extract plans and elevations and then cutout sections. I did a lot of model building before CGI [developed], so I was able to take my experience from building in the real world and bring it into CG."

Bodnarus' own computer models are not the ones that will be used later for the actual show — the task of taking the illustrator's designs and turning them into the polished, detailed scenes we see in finished episodes belongs to the visual effects department. However, before they get to work, Bodnarus does create CG models for them to work from, which enables the art department to hand over the exact proportions and style as approved by the executive producers for the VFX team to work from.

Above: The *Daedalus* was designed to suggest an aircraft carrier.

"The second part of the *Daedalus* equation was actually designing the ship itself for VFX," Bodnarus explains. "We had a concept sketch that had been done already and there was something about it that wasn't quite clicking for Brad Wright. So we talked about it and basically he ripped off half of the drawing, and said, 'I want something flat and low.' So I [asked], 'Like an aircraft carrier?' and he said, 'Yeah, like an aircraft carrier.' So we ended up designing this sort of aircraft carrier in space, which was the *Daedalus*. We kept echoes of the *Prometheus*, because I thought it was important to [do that]. We're taking the technology and building on it, and I didn't want to depart radically from the *Prometheus*."

Though the *Daedalus* is an example of his design being seen in what Bodnarus calls a 'pivotal' aspect of the show, the illustrator reports that he often finds the most pleasure in designing smaller elements over which he is often able to exercise more control. Though such elements may only appear in one episode, and for a short period of time, the design process is just as enjoyable.

One episode that particularly excited Bodnarus' illustrator talents was 'Conversion', in which he was called upon to design a concept for the Iratus bug 'egg

Below: The sleek new Earth warship, the *Daedalus*.

"DAEDALUS"
FORWARD PLANETARY DEFENCE CARRIER

sack' from which Sheppard is forced to retrieve samples. In fact, the artist's imagination was so stimulated by the idea of the episode that he'd finished his design before the production meeting was even over! "We were talking about what this egg sack should look like in a meeting," says Bodnarus with a laugh, "and as we're talking I'm drawing and listening to Brad. So once he was finished I showed him the sketch I'd done and he said, 'Yeah, like that,' so I just put some ink on it and then I issued it!"

Though only on screen for a matter of minutes as a finished article, one of the illustrator's favorite designs for season two was developed for 'The Long Goodbye'. "I think I've been most pleased with the pods for 'The Long Goodbye'. I was thinking about a 1972 Dodge, the old

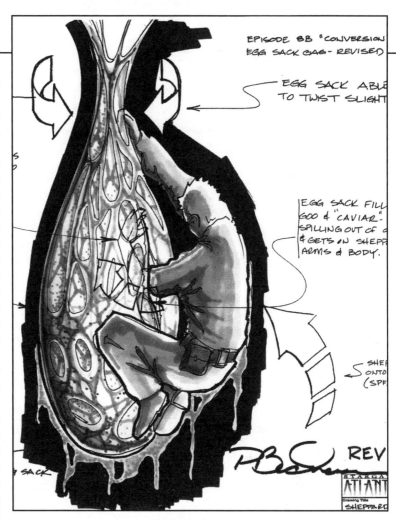

Above: The egg sack Sheppard must scale to save himself in 'Conversion'.

factory hot rods, and that led me into this kind of 'curved but angular' direction. In that situation, I started from scratch; I didn't get any direction from Brad or Bridget. I basically pitched them a concept and Bridget said, 'Sure, go with that,' and I was able to develop it. I was really proud that my first instincts really worked. I was trying to create the sense that these characters are warriors, space travelers. They're tough guys, [which] you don't realize at the time. When their consciousnesses are transferred into our characters, we imagine them to be quite benign, and then we find out that they're not. These guys are kind of bad asses, so I wanted to bring some of that out in the design of the pods! It was a really fun project because the pods themselves were beautifully made out of fiberglass by the model shop. We had a CG version and we also had a 'real' version, and the two match seamlessly. We had very nice mechanics working, very nice illuminated panels... it was just a beautifully made thing. Å

VISUAL EFFECTS

MARK SAVELA

Throughout the course of its run, *Stargate SG-1* has always set a high bar for its visual effects components, and *Stargate: Atlantis* has proven just as diligent at keeping that high standard. For season two, the production ramped up the visual effects potential of the show by introducing the *Daedalus*. Designed to serve as a link between the city of Atlantis and Earth, the ship also facilitated the sort of space-bound adventures that had not been possible for the Atlantis team in season one. Though the ship had been seen briefly in season one's finale, 'The Siege II', for season two the *Stargate: Atlantis* VFX team got to work refining the ship for closer inspection.

Mark Savela, visual effects supervisor for both *Stargate SG-1*'s season nine and *Stargate: Atlantis*' season two, recalls how the ship evolved from that first appearance onwards. "The full-on ship came about in season two," he says, "and the first time it was actually seen in all its glory was in 'Siege III', when it appears right after Caldwell comes in to save Sheppard. It's basically the next level after the *Prometheus* from *Stargate SG-1*. It was taken on as an upgrade, so it was made to look a little bit more battle-ready. It has an aircraft carrier feel to it — it's a nice looking ship."

Below: The Wraith armada attacks Atlantis.

One unique aspect of the *Daedalus* was where it was built. Whereas in previous years,
the team had overseen projects that were developed outside of Bridge Studios by VFX
vendors such as Image Engine and Rainmaker, for the show's second year the decision
was made to create an in-house VFX shop. "For season two we actually created an in-
house department as well," Savela explains. "So in addition to all our other vendors, we
also had an in-house department, with about five artists. We got off to an early start and
built the *Daedalus* in-house as a CG model. That came out of concept drawings from
James Robbins in the art department, and then they were modified and really worked on
a lot with Brad Wright to create what we finally came up with."

Although that meant that the basic CG model for the ship was built and ready to
use very early on in pre-production on the season, Savela reports that the *Daedalus* still
went through plenty of revisions following its début. "Any ship that's new you build
for establishing shots, and then as you go along we 'detail up' sections of the ship as
we go. In episode two, 'The Intruder', we get to see F-302's coming out of the cargo
bay, and we're on the top deck of the *Daedalus*, so we see all the dishes and everything
else. Those all had to be more detailed for the second episode. So ships are usually a
work in progress throughout the entire run of the series. We had a really nice shot [at
the end of the season] in 'Allies' where we're actually on the bridge of the *Daedalus*
looking out of the window with Sheppard and Caldwell. We come out of hyperspace
and we actually see the nose of the ship. We get fired on right away, which does some
nice damage to the nose. So we definitely got to have a lot of fun with the *Daedalus*!"

For Savela, having a new component like the *Daedalus* in play for season two meant
that the visual effects potential in *Stargate: Atlantis* was immediately given a boost.

"There was definitely a lot of larger-scale space battles. The Wraith hive ships are huge, and jumpers couldn't really go up against them [in season one]. The scale of the *Daedalus* compared to the hive ships isn't that large, but we have the ability to go up one-on-one against the hive ships, which is neat. Later on in the season we discover the *Aurora*, which is an Ancient ship that's very large compared to the *Daedalus*. Then we see it again in 'Inferno' and 'Allies', where it's called the *Orion*, the sister-ship to the *Aurora*. It just bumps up the scope of what you can do in terms of the battle sequences. Because in season one, it would usually be 'jumpers against darts', and in season two we could go '*Daedalus* against Hives'. It just pushes the scale up a lot to have a ship like the *Daedalus* involved."

Another important vessel in season two was the Ancient warship. First seen as the *Aurora* in the year's ninth episode, the CG ship would later be given an overhaul to become the *Orion*. Because of the nature of the ship's appearance in 'Aurora', the team had to use a round about way to develop the CG model. "When we were doing *Aurora*, we knew that a sister ship would come back, so we built the full ship and then destroyed it," Savela explains. "We actually got art department drawings of it deconstructed because they were doing concept artwork from the ['Aurora'] script. So we

Below: An F-302 launches from the Daedalus' cargo bay.

had to take those, build the entire ship and then tear it down for the show. In 'Aurora', you never actually see the outside of the ship fully done — you're just inside in the virtual world. And then when we see it later in 'Inferno' and 'Allies', it's actually built. The *Aurora/Orion* was another ship that we actually built in house as a CG model and we [also] did all of the space shots for *Aurora* in house, as well."

For Savela, the effects that he and the rest of the VFX team produced for the end of *Stargate: Atlantis'* second season were the highlight of the year. "I think 'Allies' was the coolest, because it was written to be continued. It was a neat show to do because there was the 'F-302 in space' stuff, which is really fun to explore. We did it in 'Intruder', where we had the unmanned F-302 against Sheppard and McKay's F-302, which I think was really cool. And then we got to do four against a couple of Hives and a wave of Darts in 'Allies'. The F-302 looks really nice and we get to incorporate production shots because we do have the F-302 on stage as well. I like to incorporate Sheppard in the cockpit [with the external VFX shots] to really blend it in, so we get to see his actions inside the cockpit as well. It's tricky, but it's fun and well worth it. It's those shots that I like the best, because it really ties the live action into the CG, so it doesn't give it away that it's a full-on VFX shot. It's hard to keep those shots really fresh when you rely on these big, wide 100 per cent CG shots that are just ships doing battle in space. That's been the real challenge for us, because everyone in the world has seen space battles so many times by now, and it's about trying to keep the camera angles and the moves fresh. You try to put a different eye to it." Å

Above: The *Orion* prepares for launch to escape the 'Inferno'.

MAKE-UP SPECIAL EFFECTS

TODD MASTERS

Few aspects of *Stargate: Atlantis* are more striking than the special make-up effects used to create the show's alien characters, in particular the terrifying look of the Wraith. Though mostly designed in-house by the production's talented art team at Bridge Studios, these creatures are brought to life by Todd Masters and his award-winning team. For *Stargate: Atlantis'* second season, they found themselves charged with developing some of the most stunning effects yet, largely revolving around the evolution of the Wraith. Early in the season, the team was given the task of creating a new-style look for a young Wraith girl. With the appearance of Ellia (Jewel Stait) in 'Instinct' the audience was introduced to a different, somewhat softer, side of the predators so feared throughout the Pegasus Galaxy.

"She was supposed to look a lot younger, like a teenager," Masters explains, of their design brief for Ellia, "so the idea was to make her softer. The design that the art department did had her face a lot rounder than she was, and so we had to make some choices with that. Then when she turned into the monster, that was again an art department design that we matched. What we wanted to do originally [for that] was an animatronic mask. But for budget and schedule reasons we had to do a prosthetic. It was a complicated piece to do. We had to do both make-ups at the same time, because they [only] shot for five days. So we had to work on her subtle Wraith make-up as well as her big monster make-up at the same time — and at the same time creating her body suit! She had this part-bug body suit, coordinated with her wardrobe, contact lenses, hair — the whole deal. So it was quite a big deal to do in five days!"

Another challenge that arose on the shoot of 'Instinct' was creating and maintaining the make-up for Ellia's six-year old self, played by child actor Kayma Seamark. Spending hours putting prosthetics on a trained actor is one thing — getting a child to even sit still long enough to fit the make-up is something else entirely! "She was very young, and she was very patient for the first couple of hours," laughs Masters, recalling the day. "We had designed this prosthetic to go on really quickly and film really quickly so we'd get the little person out of there in record time — she was really young, so she could only shoot for so many hours. So we got it on her and she really loved it, she looked fantastic. And then hours went by and she got impatient, and she started to get bored, and then she fell asleep on it! My poor make-up artist on set, Celine Godeau, was freaking out. She was like, 'It looked great for so long and now we're going to shoot and it's barely holding up!' But I think it looked great in the show. At the time it was, 'Oh my god, that was the perfect make-up... *eight hours ago!*'" Masters laughs again, remaining philosophical. "But that's one of the many things that go on in production. There's always some sort of situation to deal with on any day. But she was a good little young lady."

'Instinct' in turn led into 'Conversion', which saw star Joe Flanigan experiencing the first prosthetics of his career. The episode also brought another challenge for Masters and his team, as they were called upon to evolve a bug-like make-up effect to match the beginnings that had been seen in the previous episode. "There was lots of make-up in 'Conversion', and it was fantastic to work with Joe," recalls the make-up artist. "We didn't really know each other that well — obviously we had seen each other on the lot, but we'd never really crossed paths or talked much. So this was funny, because you never really know how an actor is going to be in these situations. It's early morning, we've got the cold glue and the smelly bits [of prosthetic] and all that! But he was fantastic, he was really into it. I think he secretly liked it a lot more than he let on! He looked really cool in it."

Part of the reason the finished make-up was so effective, in Masters eyes, was that it grew throughout the episode, becoming more and more apparent as the story went on. "There were a couple of different stages. Some were just bites on his arm, and then a whole hand got transformed, and then it kind of worked up his body. So we got to work out, in different stages of that script, how this disease would take over his body. I think Joe really appreciated that, it helped him figure out the character and what he was going through. Ultimately, for the final stage, he was wearing two hands, the neck and the face pieces that were translucent so that we could under-paint them and show this stuff coursing beneath his skin. He had lenses too, so it was quite a fun transformation."

Much later in the season, the design and transformation work that Masters and his team had worked on for 'Conversion' came into play again, for the second season's most shocking episode — 'Michael', with guest star Connor Trinneer. "There's so many great things that we're doing on the show, but I really liked the stuff we did in 'Michael'. That was exciting for us," he says. "First, we loved the script, it was our favorite of last year. It was a nice challenge. We knew that the storyline where the Wraith were going to be humanized was coming but we didn't realize this was the original script, and it was cool, doing all the stages. We had already done the episode where Joe transforms, so we already had some designs worked out. It was fun to see where the human design meets the Wraith design. We didn't have as many stages as we did on Joe's episode — we had this kind of fifty/fifty Wraith/Human prosthetic that we used quite a bit. He looked really dashing in that. I thought that was a great look for him."

Above: Ellia, a different kind of Wraith for Masters' team to create.

MAKE-UP SPECIAL EFFECTS

The make-up for Michael became more complicated later in the season, with the character's return in 'Allies'. Though the character was the same, Masters and his team discovered that because of Connor Trinneer's unavailability, they would have to perform the make-up on a different actor, Brent Stait, better known to viewers as Ferretti in *Stargate SG-1* and Rev Bem in *Gene Rodenberry's Andromeda*. Since Connor Trinneer would be returning in season three to play the character, Stait's make-up had to be made to look as close to the original Michael as possible. This meant that Masters had to use the same cast created from Trinneer's face, and mould it to Stait's features, thus keeping as much of the outward character prosthetic as possible.

"Yeah, talk about confusion! It was Brent Stait playing Connor playing Michael," Masters laughs. "We did a cast on Brent. We already had [the cast of Connor] and we had the make-up that we did on Connor, and fortunately Brent and Connor have similar features. But we also took some license, because he was to have evolved to another state. So we went a little more Wraith."

This evolution of the Wraith face is something that Masters would like to have more chance to do. Since most of the Wraith characters are played by the same actors, introducing differences is something of a challenge — though a welcome one. "We changed things behind the scenes, and technique, for season two. As far as the design goes we didn't really change anything that much in terms of the overall Wraith design. We stopped using the necks in certain cases. Originally, the Wraith had heads and necks that were a little tighter than was comfortable [for the actors]. But we didn't really change much of the design. As different stories came along we did certain things, like Michael — that was a whole different character so we had a chance to change him. I love to do more Wraith designs, to get variety into those characters."

Masters is also quick to praise the regular Wraith actors beneath the make-up — for example James Lafazanos, Geoff Redknap and Andie Frizzell. "The Wraith are a lot of fun. They are a challenge to do at times but they are fun. But it is tough — and I'm speaking more from the make-up side because that's what I know. I can't even imagine getting up early in the morning and having a bunch of crazy people throw goo on your face and contact lenses in your eyes and big fangs in your mouth before it's even eight o'clock! They should get prizes for that!"

Below: Star Joe Flanigan gets his first taste of prosthetics.

One of these regular returnees in the shape of a Wraith is Andie Frizzell, first seen in *Stargate: Atlantis*' pilot episode 'Rising' as the Wraith Queen. She is still going strong in the show's second year, appearing as two different Wraith Queens, in the mid-season two-parter 'The Lost Boys' and 'The Hive', and in the shocking finale, 'Allies'.

"Andie is a great actress," Masters enthuses. "She is quite the actress under rubber! It's one thing to work your own face, it's another to work through a couple of inches of someone else's face! It's based on the initial Queen Wraith mold, which Andie played as well, and we just reworked, redressed certain aspects of it [for the different Queens]. At first she had this really crazy red hair, which I loved. I thought that was really vital for the show, very punk. And then we went to white, and she had a mixed hair in the last one. So it's like a leopard or a panther — they look similar but they are different. That's kind of the idea for the species."

Having worked with the pressures of television production for many years, Masters knows what challenges to expect in trying to create such marvelous make-up effects to a strict schedule. However, during the second year of *Stargate: Atlantis*, whilst simultaneously producing make-up for *Stargate SG-1*, the one thing Masters wished for was more time. "In season two it was getting a little ridiculous, because they kept doing these episodes and there would suddenly be a script in my box — and fortunately we would be checking our boxes all the time, because you start reading a new script and you're like, 'Okay… this plays in a *week*?' This stuff isn't on a shelf somewhere, we have to custom build it each time. I think I'm going to wear a shirt at meetings from now on," he jokes, "'Prosthetics are done by humans!'" Å

BOB AKESTER

Though most of the viewers attention is focused on the television screen, quite often the first inkling of what can be expected from an upcoming episode comes courtesy of Bob Akester's stills photography. Since *Stargate: Atlantis'* pilot episode, Akester has spent much time on set, shooting the publicity stills that will be used the world over to promote the show. Far from simply grabbing the best shots he can, however, the photographer has made it his mission to create the most exciting images he can, images that reflect exactly what *Stargate: Atlantis* is all about.

"I like to get away from the scenes where they are just standing around and talking," Akester explains. "I like to shoot when they have lots of action, and I want to get the actors doing something so that visually you can see them doing something — running around and fighting, flying airplanes… That just adds so much more value to it, and if I can add some CG to it that makes it more sci-fi, then I like to do that."

One particular CG element that the photographer adds to his images is the Stargate 'kawoosh' action. Normally, of course, anyone taking a picture of filming that involves the Stargate would only see the ring, probably with the CG-ready 'green screen' standing behind it. Akester, however, will use the digital images he takes in

Below: Catching the stunt-men in mid-flight.

Above: One of season two's bigger explosions.

these circumstances merely as a base for the finished print, and work on it in his studio so that when the public finally see the picture, it will appear complete — 'kawoosh' and all.

"The CG guys give me the artwork and then I combine it into my image. So if there's green screen there I will take it and use a software called Primatt to remove the green and insert the image. It can be tricky," he continues, "the software requires me to be very precise. But all of it is based on Photoshop, and that's a great platform to start from. You just get all these plug-ins to do all the extra work that you need. So it's basically layers that you create yourself and submit that as the final image. I do as many as I can. Time is always a constraint, because I do probably fifty gigabytes of images a week. And that's a lot of images! You end up not being able to do as many as you would like, so I try to do the ones that are key story pieces."

Something that has made Akester's life easier in this regard is the advent and development of digital photographic technology, as he explains: "The reason I like digital is a lot of times there are things on set that catch on the edge [of the image], like marks on the floor, microphones, or even just bits of set. With digital I can improve it instead of having to compromise my composition, like you used to have to do with film. Film was always limiting in that regard. Also you can see when you've got something really interesting when you're using digital. With film, you have to keep shooting and you end up with a lot more than you need. With digital you can shoot just a few frames and there's the key piece, I've got it and I can walk away and start worrying about another angle. So digital makes that really easy."

Akester's determination to get the best shot possible sometimes means putting himself in harms way. Since safety is of paramount importance on the sets at Bridge Studios — and the photographer knows from personal experience just how dangerous some situations can be — he always works with the stunt coordinator on set to work out the best position for his camera. "Safety is really highly regarded on the sets in Vancouver especially," says Akester. "I remember when I did a John Frankenheimer film called *Dead Bang* and they were firing shotguns in a cave, I used to get gunpowder on my arms and it would sting. Now, they won't even let me get close to those kind of positions! I was on a set once when somebody got the restrictor of a prop-gun embedded into his liver. He was quite badly injured.

"So what they do now is, I talk specifically to the armorer way before the actual shooting starts taking place, so that he and I can have a conversation when he's not under pressure. I'll say 'This is what I want to get, am I okay here?' And he'll say, 'No,' and he makes a suggestion and I may accept that or make another suggestion. I have a Lexon shield that I carry with me so that I can hide behind that, so that I'm protected. I make sure my hearing protection is on and I sometimes put a hardhat on. So I try to be very careful with that, because of that one instance — I'm pretty nervous

Right: One of Akester's 'widescreen' photos, taken during a break in filming on 'Inferno'.

about making sure it's right! And because of the trust I've gained with the armorers, they know who I am and they know I'm not going to be stupid, so they let me get into places that they don't let a lot of other people get into. So I'm pretty lucky that way. I'm willing to curl up in a corner and get dirty. My wife figures I haven't been to work if I don't come home dirty!" laughs Akester. "If I've got mud all over me, she'll say 'Oh, you've been at work today, haven't you?'"

Stargate: Atlantis has also afforded the photographer the chance to experiment with different styles of stills images, particularly within the digital environment. "What really got me excited in the first season was the panoramics I started doing," he explains. "It was something that I had never tried before, because digital was so clunky at that time. So I thought, 'Well, why not try this?' So I started trying it with the sets and then I started combining it to make it a more interesting ratio, more of a movie ratio: 16:9. So then I started making these compositions. Sometimes it's two frames, sometimes it's sixteen frames. And that really got me excited. 16:9 is the ratio of high definition [film and video]. So I try to get the same ratio as seen in HD, because it's a very cool ratio, it's more natural than you have with the standard 35mm camera. In fact, it's even better than the regular television frame. When I first started, they all wanted vertical. But with the Internet, horizontal now seems to be quite acceptable — you get to see the whole frame instead of having to scroll down." Å

WRAPPING SEASON TWO

I've been visiting the Bridge Studios since *Stargate SG-1* was filming its sixth season, and when *Stargate: Atlantis* went into production, my semi-regular visits expanded to take in that side of the lot too. There are few more bustling places on Earth than a film set in full swing. It's not glamorous, as some might expect from the appendages of fame that go with working on a high-profile series. It's plain hard work and graft from dawn till dusk — but generally, along with the effort, there's a lot of fun, too. Each day progresses with an air of barely-restrained chaos as hundreds of crew members work through the constant cycle of setting up for a shot, doing their assigned tasks in a frenzy of activity until the cameras are ready to roll, and falling into an immediate and complete hush as filming begins. Then, as soon as that shot is in the can, the cycle starts all over again. A film set is a place of energy, unrelenting effort and — if both cast and crew are lucky — happy camaraderie. Every production hopes for harmony when they start a new show, and with *Stargate: Atlantis*, they've certainly found it.

Today, the energy levels on *Stargate: Atlantis* have multiplied a thousand fold, for this is the day that the show wraps on its second year of episodes. Despite the amount of visits I've racked up over the previous seasons, this is the first time I've had the privilege of being present at a season wrap. Usually, the final week of filming is too hectic to allow journalists in to observe. Unlike earlier in the shooting year, when both first and second unit directors can rely on squeezing some time in somewhere later to finish a shot they didn't make on their own schedule, the final week of filming is as final as it gets. And as you can imagine, when it gets to the final day of filming — well, let's just say that every cast and crew member comes to work on that day preparing to work extra long hours.

There is a lot of work to do, everyone needs to be focused to achieve their respective goals, and yet despite that (and the knowledge that today they'll have to keep filming until everything's done, no matter how late shooting runs) there is an undeniable party atmosphere hanging over the set. It's like the last day of school before a vacation. Everyone here has been working their butts off for the past nine months to get twenty episodes of top television in the can... and in a few hours, they will have wrapped them all completely. As I arrive on set at 10am, three hours after the main cast were called to set, I can almost taste the excitement in the air.

Director Peter DeLuise and first assistant director Alex Pappas can't wait to wrap either, but neither of them can get into the party spirit until the last few scenes of 'Inferno' are in the can, and that's a long day's work away yet. Though the penultimate episode to air, 'Inferno' is the last episode to film, with 'Allies' having wrapped principle shooting a week earlier. With a big finale, the director and crew need as much time as possible to pick up stray shots, so generally the last two episodes of the season are switched to allow some 'wiggle room' on the schedules.

About to go before the camera are Torri Higginson's last scenes of the season,

Above: Video Village.

which are being filmed on the Effects Stage, colloquially known as the 'Blade III' set, because some of *Stargate: Atlantis'* standing sets were built on and around an existing set left over from the movie *Blade: Trinity*. Upstairs is the 'Chair Room', which used to house the Ancient drone chair, but the set decoration department has worked their magic to transform it into Chancellor Lycos' office on Taranis. The last scene to be filmed up here is the argument in which Lycos accuses Weir of wanting to steal Taranis' Ancient warship.

Video Village (the term for the collection of television and computer screens from which the director and his team monitor proceedings) is situated just outside the set doorway. From here, Peter DeLuise is watching his crew set up, and checking camera angles whilst fiddling with a lump of plastic. On closer inspection, this turns out to be an old *Stargate SG-1* calculator with which the producers had been presented some years previously. The director explains that it hasn't worked for ages, but he noticed it on his shelf earlier. It used to have black plastic fins along each side (why the calculators had these is anyone's guess, they don't look at all *Stargate*-ish), but these have now been pulled off.

"Look out for this," DeLuise instructs, mock-seriously. "I needed some buttons for the *Orion*'s chair. I think they'll work perfectly." He then presents me with the calculator. "You take it. It'll make a good competition prize. Or I bet someone will buy it on eBay." The calculator, still finless, has now found a permanent home in my living room. When I watched the episode later, sure enough, there was Sheppard pressing

Peter DeLuise's makeshift buttons on the newly named *Orion*'s control chair. Ah, the wonders of high production value television…

Having finished setting up, the crew move off the set and the cameras roll on Higginson's final scene of the season. A couple of smooth takes later and DeLuise yells, "Cut! And that's an episode wrap for Kevin McNulty [Chancellor Lycos] and a season wrap for Torri Higginson!" Applause rattles around the set from everyone on the crew as the actress begins to hug people goodbye. The hugging will go on all day — it takes a lot of people to put a series like *Stargate: Atlantis* together, and over the last nine months the cast and crew have become very close. Some of them won't be returning, which makes the goodbye even more poignant.

With that scene complete, it's time to move directly downstairs to the *Orion* bridge set, where DeLuise and the crew will be filming more scenes from 'Inferno'. This time the actors due on set are Joe Flanigan, David Hewlett, Rachel Luttrell, Jason Momoa, Paul McGillion and guest star Brandy Ledford (Norina).

It's now 11am, and the crew have been filming for about four-and-a-half hours. It's not time for lunch yet, but people are certainly hungry. Not only that, it's late September in Vancouver, BC, and even with the studio lights, it's chilly. So when craft services arrive with a very large canister of hot, nourishing chicken and rice soup, everyone is happy. Meanwhile, grips bustle around getting a mass of equipment into position. Once everything is ready, Pappas uses his radio to call the second assistant

Below: Higginson and Flanigan in full swing.

director, stationed outside at the 'circus' (the slang term for the trucks that congregate around any film set, comprised of make-up trailers, actors trailers, guest cast quarters and so on), and ask that the required actors be called to set.

This is the set that the cast and crew will be filming in for the rest of the day as they block shoot everything that takes place on the *Orion*'s bridge. Scripts aren't filmed chronologically. Instead, executive producer N. John Smith, who has the mammoth task of scheduling each and every episode of both *Stargate: Atlantis* and *Stargate SG-1*, has to make sure that each set change is as minimal as possible. This means that today DeLuise will be filming scenes set on the *Orion* bridge from throughout the 'Inferno' script.

The main cast arrive on set, Joe Flanigan carrying two huge boxes. As the crew hush, the actor explains that they're full of pastries that he and his wife wanted the crew to enjoy as a thank you for all their hard work that year. Or at least, they had at one time been

full — someone's already had a nibble. Still, there's plenty to go around, and as the cast settle into their places and discuss the scene with DeLuise before a quick rehearsal, three grips set up some tables at the back to house the pastries. The crew waste no time in tucking in, and soon everyone is munching happily (again). Wrap days, as I was to learn later at lunch, involve a *lot* of food.

Filming begins again, but the crew, who have been buoyed even more by Flanigan's gesture, are noisy, and though this may be only in relative terms, it's enough to disrupt the take. They can't seem to settle, which is particularly unusual for a Vancouver crew that has been working together for so long. Canada is renowned for having some of the best film workers in the industry, and for them to be so distracted is an indication of the 'cabin fever' that's struck the set today. DeLuise calls cut for a reset twice before Alex Pappas, who has clearly had enough of the interruptions, stands on a wooden box and shouts to get everyone's attention. The annoyed second assistant director tells everyone present in no uncertain terms that the next person to make a noise will be sent off the stage. A couple of minutes later, the crew is finally able to settle and filming begins again.

At 1pm, the company breaks for lunch. Outside, it's pouring with rain, but nothing seems to be able to dampen the crew's spirits today as they queue for what they know will be the best craft menu of the year. The standard of food at Bridge — in fact, on every set in North America — is extremely high, but today, of course, is a special day. There's fillet steak and lobster on the menu, along with strawberries dipped in chocolate and the most amazing gateaux I've ever seen. How anyone stays in shape on a film set, especially *this* film set, is beyond me.

Everyone, including Torri Higginson and Joe Flanigan, piles into the tent with their lunch. Generally the main cast will eat in their trailers, learning lines and preparing for the next scene. But today is different, today is a day for taking a step back and looking at everything around them — it may be completely different when the production comes back for season three. In the world of television, changes can be unexpected, unpredictable and fast. Best to catch your breath and say your thank yous and goodbyes while you have the opportunity... just in case.

After lunch, filming continues apace. Mid-afternoon sees the series wrap for Jason Momoa and Rachel Luttrell. Momoa, who has been suffering with a severe cold all week, lets out a great 'whoop' and squeezes Luttrell in a huge bear hug before they both make their way off set so that filming can continue as quickly as possible. In the darkness between takes shortly afterwards, director Andy Mikita arrives and has a quick word with Peter DeLuise. Mikita, who has just finished filming over on Stage Six, helmed the season finale, 'Allies', and there are a couple of pickup shots that he's

Below: McKay just wants to do his job.

hoping DeLuise can fit in for him. The two confer about what directing approach they need to take before the extras for the scene arrive and the filming recommence.

As 6pm approaches — filming has now been underway for eleven hours — the production staff, whose day is ending, begin to filter into the set. Though the producers and post-production staff (which includes editing and VFX) will continue to work at Bridge for some weeks to come, this is the last opportunity they will have to see the cast and crew this year. Director Martin Wood arrives, as do executive producers Brad Wright and Robert Cooper. Executive producer Joe Mallozzi pops in, and co-producer Martin Gero comes to joke with DeLuise. They're all incredibly tired, but very happy with the season. As a team they've managed to turn out forty episodes of television, *Stargate: Atlantis* and *Stargate SG-1* (which is currently wrapping about a hundred yards away on Stage Two), so they have a right to be proud of their accomplishments.

Above: Higginson shoots one of her last scenes for season two.

The producers gradually melt away, and still filming continues. The minutes tick by. As the crew move on to the last scene, rumor has it that the place to be for a party after wrap is the lighting truck. There is talk of margaritas ready to be made, or whatever else you might fancy after a long, hard season of work. Personally, as I stand there clutching a cup of tea, I'm already ready for bed, and I've done nothing except take notes and conduct interviews all day. These crew members are a hardy lot, to be sure.

Between setups, Alex Pappas sees me standing in the corner, notebook in hand, and comes over. We've met several times and, like most of the crew, he's got used to me as a bit of set furniture when I visit. He's a funny, warm man with neat white hair and an organized air. His outburst earlier was as unusual as the crew failing to settle.

"What are you taking notes about this time?" he asks, indicating my pen and paper.

"Just about wrapping the season," I reply.

He grimaces. "You didn't see me yell earlier, did you? I hope you didn't make any notes about that…" One of the grips nearby laughs.

"Of course not!" I say innocently, with a reassuring smile.

At 8.30pm, thirteen-and-a-half hours after filming started for the day, Peter DeLuise yells "Cut" on *Stargate: Atlantis* for the final time in season two. A great cheer goes up, and the hugging and shaking of hands begins all over again. On the set, a tired Joe Flanigan embraces Peter DeLuise, and I decide it's time to head for my hotel.

I get in a few hugs of my own on the way out. It's a TV tradition, apparently. Å

AFTERWORD

S o, when I was asked to write this Afterword, my first response was, "Uhm… shouldn't Brad be doing this?"

"No," I was told, "he did it last year."

"Oh, okay, well… shouldn't Rob write the Afterword then?"

"No," I was told, "he's doing *SG-1*."

"Ah," I said, "well, what about having the cast write something?"

"They're doing the Foreword."

"I see… So basically everyone has said no, so you're asking me?"

"Yes," I was told, after an uncomfortable pause.

So, as the last resort, it is my great privilege to write the final page in this very comprehensive look back at season two…

The first year of a new TV show is always a bumpy one (I've only been a part of one show, but that's what I hear). When I was originally hired, production had already begun on the pilot and there was only one other script ready to go, so the whole year was a race to stay ahead of the production. All the while trying to find the voices of these new characters, and figuring out how to make our show different enough from *SG-1* so it wasn't a clone and familiar enough so it wouldn't alienate fans. We made some mistakes, but under Brad and Rob's steady hands we eventually made more good episodes than bad… Heck, some were even pretty great.

Coming into the second year, we had more confidence, more money and most importantly more time to come up with stories. Writing on *Stargate* is truly a collaborative process. By the time a script is ready to be prepped, everyone has put their mark on it. In fact, without fail, when people come up and say, "Oh man, such and such a line was my fave," it has inevitably been the one thing that some other writer has come up with… Brad is famous for adding that one line to everyone's script that you wish you could take credit for (and do when he's not around).

Now, you can have written the best script in the world but if you don't have world-class directors, cast and crew the show's gonna suck. I always figure that what I imagine in my head when I'm writing will certainly be better than what we can actually do… but I'm almost always wrong. Whether it be a great set, an amazing camera move or an actor's unique take on a line, the team of people here always makes me look better than I am and consistently exceeds my expectations.

As I write this, I've just handed over this year's mid-season two-parter to Brad so he can do his draft… None of season three has aired, so there's always that nagging "Will they like this?" feeling in the back of our mind. It's a nerve-wracking time.

I gotta say though, even after reading all the drafts of a script, sitting through countless production meetings, watching seemingly endless hours of dailies, when we finally get that first mix back and see the show all together for the first time, I always think to my self, "Yeah... I'd watch this show."

You bought this book, so I assume you agree. Å

MARTIN GERO
Producer
Vancouver, May 2006

GATE ADVENTURES!

- ◎ **Exclusive interviews with the cast of** *Stargate SG-1* **&** *Stargate: Atlantis*!
- ◎ **Show directors, writers & producers debriefed!**
- ◎ **All the latest news on both shows!**

ALSO AVAILABLE FROM
TITAN BOOKS
Illustrated Companion series

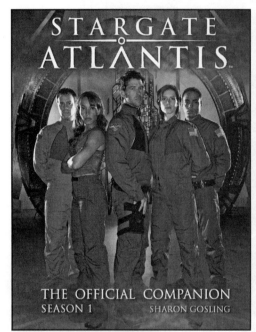

STARGATE ATLANTIS
THE OFFICIAL COMPANION
SEASON 1   SHARON GOSLING

STARGATE SG·1
THE ILLUSTRATED COMPANION
SEASONS 1 AND 2   Thomasina Gibson

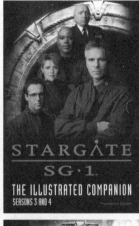

STARGATE SG·1
THE ILLUSTRATED COMPANION
SEASONS 3 AND 4   Thomasina Gibson

STARGATE SG·1
THE ILLUSTRATED COMPANION
SEASONS 5 AND 6   Thomasina Gibson

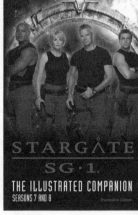

STARGATE SG·1
THE ILLUSTRATED COMPANION
SEASONS 7 AND 8   Thomasina Gibson

STARGATE SG·1
THE ILLUSTRATED COMPANION
SEASON 9   Sharon Gosling

COMING SOON!
Stargate SG-1: The Illustrated Companion Season 9

WWW.TITANBOOKS.COM